Shakespeare's Sonnets

Martin Seymour-Smith

GREENWICH EXCHANGE
LONDON

Greenwich Exchange, London

Student Guide to Shakespeare's Sonnets

Printed and bound by Quorn Selective Repro Ltd, Loughborough
Tel: 01509 213456
Typesetting and layout by Albion Associates, London
Tel: 020 8852 4646

Greenwich Exchange Website: www.greenex.co.uk

ISBN 1-871551-38-2

CONTENTS

ACKNOWLEDLEDGEMENTS
TO FIRST EDITION

I WISH to thank the following: Roger Sharrock, for reading and helpfully annotating the first part of a draft of this edition, and for pointing out some errors; James Reeves, for advice and encouragement at every stage; the staff of both the Finchley and the Bexhill Public Libraries, for their courteous and unfailing assistance in obtaining difficult books; my parents, Andrew Mylett, A. H. Rees and Mrs Heather Karolyi for invaluable help with proofs and for saving me from errors; and Janet Seymour-Smith.

M. S-S
Bexhill-on-Sea, Sussex
1963

PREFACE

This old spelling edition of *Shakespeare's Sonnets* was first published by Heinemann in 1963. It was revised by Martin Seymour-Smith and myself in 1998. As Seymour-Smith convincingly demonstrates, the return to the text as originally spelt reveals layers of meaning which are lost in a modernised version. In such a concentrated, ambiguous, ironical and inward-looking sequence as the *Sonnets* is, this matters in a way that does necessarily apply to Shakespeare's plays.

In his introduction and notes Martin Seymour-Smith traces Shakespeare's mental odyssey as he passes through an acute psychological crisis, facing up to unexpected – and unwelcome – truths about his sexual desires. His commentary on the progress of the relationship between Shakespeare and the Friend demonstrates the passage from an idealised Renaissance love between men, through a relationship with a homosexual dimension which undoubtedly deeply disturbs the poet, to a disillusion which, however, Shakespeare never allows to descend to disgust, nor even uses to dismiss the Friend out of hand. A record of painful honesty, the *Sonnets* provide virtually the only direct glimpse we have into one aspect of Shakespeare's personal life.

Peter Davies,
Twickenham
2000

INTRODUCTION

1

SHAKESPEARE'S SONNETS have had much learned ink wasted upon them, and in this Introduction I can offer little more than a summary of the facts and theories that have been regarded as important.

One of the reasons for the enduring fame of the *Sonnets* is that, appearing to be on an intensely personal and even 'forbidden' theme, they therefore seem to cast light on the personality, largely hidden from history, of their author. A better reason is that they represent a unique combination of inspired linguistic wit and depth of passionate feeling. It is no wonder that nearly everyone who reads them with attention finds himself unable to resist the temptation of projecting himself, and therefore his own theories and predilections, into them. The critic or scholar can only claim to have tried to be objective in his treatment: they are too profound, too wide in their emotional and psychological range, to obtain dispassionate treatment. At best, an editor can hope for no more than to cast some light by discussion of certain of the more important facets of their meaning, and of their vocabulary. The best, and there arc many, possess such poetic robustness, such tough authenticity, that their subtlety, both linguistic and psychological, is unbounded. They are as near to life as poetry can get, and as remote. Close examination of such 'hackneyed' lines as

> What potions have I drunke of *Syren* teares
> Distil'd from Lymbecks foule as hell within,
> Applying feares to hopes, and hopes to feares,
> Still loosing when I saw my selfe to win?

which are absolute in their purely emotional appeal, proves their intellectual precision to be as intense in its hardness as their passion is intense in its heat. Any attempted assessment of such passages – and they abound – consists, in essence, of a series of re-quotations with different emphases.

In no other poems are we brought so close to ourselves; we should be content with this, and not imagine that our opinions of our experiences reflect Shakespeare's personality. Although the 'story' behind the *Sonnets,* the events that occasioned them, is clear and simple to see, at least in most of its details, personality *qua* personality is remarkably absent from the account they give. Shakespeare never points to himself and says: 'Look, this is what I was like in this situation! Look at me and admire me! See how I suffered!' He transcends this. His poems say, instead: 'Look at *you*!'

2

The Sonnet (its name derives from an Italian word meaning 'a little sound') originated in thirteenth-century Italy; the first important poet to use the form was Dante. Petrarch, who wrote the first considerable sonnet-sequence, followed Dante in preferring the rhyme scheme *abba abba cde cde.*

Sir Thomas Wyatt started writing sonnets in English after a visit to Italy in 1527; the forms of his sonnets remain close to the Italian, but within this pattern he often introduced a concluding couplet: *abba abba cdd cee*. But it is Wyatt's contemporary, a much inferior poet, the Earl of Surrey, who seems to have 'invented' what is now quite erroneously called the 'Shakespearean form': *abab cdcd efef gg*. This form of sonnet, or one near to it, is more suited to English: although Milton and others produced technically successful Petrarchan sonnets of a more generalized kind, the Italian is too artificial and restricting to allow of the sort of dramatic impact and personal immediacy to be found in Shakespeare's sonnets.

In the twenty-five years after the publication of *Tottel's Miscellany* (1557), which contained most of the sonnets of Wyatt and Surrey, and of imitators, no sonnets seem to have been written. Then, in

1582, Sir Philip Sidney wrote *Astrophel and Stella,* which, with Spenser's still underrated *Amoretti,* represents the most substantial sonnet-sequence in English next to Shakespeare. Sidney's sonnets in *Astrophel and Stella* are, in fact, technically nearer the Italian form than the Shakespearean; but the resemblance is misleading. Although he tries to follow Petrarch rather than Surrey, Sidney produces a characteristically English poem, in which the epigrammatic pull of the final couplet is the dominating factor.

A pirated edition of *Astrophel and Stella* was published in 1591, and began a period of sonneteering so intense that by 1600 it had almost burned itself out. Drayton (and perhaps Shakespeare, if any of his known sonnets belongs to the seventeenth century) was the only poet of note who continued to add to his sequence.

Most of the sonnets of this final decade of the sixteenth century are in Shakespearean form, or variants of it; all are dwarfed by Sidney, Spenser and Samuel Daniel, whose sequence *Delia* must have been one of Shakespeare's models.

A comparison between *Delia* and Shakespeare's sequence is instructive. It should be clear from the first eighteen sonnets that at the outset Shakespeare was ambitiously setting out to write a successful sequence in the accepted style of his day. But by Sonnet 20 the situation, and consequently the whole poetic atmosphere, has changed. Beginning by taking Daniel as his model, Shakespeare ends by transcending him. Unfair though this must seem to admirers of Daniel, the difference between *Delia* and the *Sonnets* is the difference between verse, albeit good verse, and poetry. Technique and procedure have ceased to matter in the Shakespeare sequence.

3

The publisher of the *Sonnets,* Thomas Thorpe, secured a licence at Stationers' Hall on 20 May 1609. This first Quarto edition (hereinafter called Q) probably appeared within a short time of its registration. But apart from a likely passing reference to the fact of publication by William Drummond of Hawthornden in about 1614, there is no known allusion from the time of registration until John Benson's edition, dated 1640, but published in 1639.

However, in 1598 a Cambridge schoolmaster and cleric. Francis Meres, who was then living in London, and certainly on familiar terms with some literary men, wrote in *Palladis Tamia*: *Wit*: *Treasury*: 'As the soul of Euphorbus was thought to live in Pythagoras: so the sweete wittie soule of *Ovid* lives in the mellifluous & hony-tongued *Shakespeare,* witnes his *Venus and Adonis,* his *Lucrece,* his sugred *Sonnets* among his private friends, &c.' Elsewhere in this book Meres listed Shakespeare as one of 'the most passionate among us to bewaile and bemoane the perplexities of Love'. It has been pointed out, fairly, that the 'sugred' *Sonnets* to which Meres referred need not be those of Q. However, he probably meant at least some of them, because in the next year, 1599, versions of two (138 and 144) appeared in a miscellaneous collection of poems, *The Passionate Pilgrim,* published by William Jaggard, the contents of which were incorrectly ascribed to Shakespeare on the title-page. In fact, only the two sonnets and three excerpts from *Love's Labour's Lost* are certainly Shakespeare's.

In 1600 Eleazar Edgar registered 'a booke called Amours by J.D. with certen oy^{r} sonnetes by W.S.'; but it is not extant, and may never have been printed, so we do not know if 'W.S.' meant Shakespeare (perhaps in association with Donne or Davies).

Thirteen copies of Q have survived, which means that it is very rare for an early seventeenth-century book. Of these, seven have the imprint of John Wright, four of William Aspley, and two lack title-pages. Evidently the edition was divided between the two booksellers, Aspley and Wright, and the imprint was varied accordingly. The printer, who had already been responsible for the Quarto of *Troilus and Cressida* (a poorish text), was George Eld; the publisher was Thomas Thorpe. Curiously enough, of the four people associated in this venture, the publisher, Thorpe, was the only one who never achieved a permanent position in the book trade. The other three were already better established than he would ever be; and in 1623 Aspley, who had been co-publisher of two of

Shakespeare's Quartos in 1600, joined the syndicate that published the First Folio. Thorpe, on the other hand, although the publisher of Marlowe's translation of Lucan's *Pharsalia,* and of Jonson's *Sejanus* and *Volpone,* remained a speculative procurer of MSS; certainly he never established a sound reputation. He died in an almshouse at Ewelme in 1634.

The title-page of the British Museum Grenville copy of Q reads: 'SHARE-SPEARES/SONNETS./Never before Imprinted./AT LONDON/By *G.Eld* for *T. T.* and are/to be solde by *William Aspley/* 1609.' There follows a dedication, signed 'T.T.', which reads as follows: 'TO. THE. ONLIE. BEGETTER. OF./THESE. INSUING. SONNETS./Mr. W.H. ALL. HAPPINESSE./AND. THAT. ETERNITIE./PROMISED./BY./OUR. EVER-LIVING. POET./ WISHETH./ THE. WELL-WISHING./ADVENTURER. IN./ SETTING./FORTH./T. T.' This is followed by one hundred and fifty-four numbered sonnets. Although it is not mentioned on the title-page, the volume ends with a poem in forty-seven stanzas of rhyme-royal headed 'A Lovers Complaint./BY/WILLIAM SHAKESPEARE.' C.S. Lewis, in his *English Literature in the Sixteenth Century,* calls this 'a still-born *chanson d'aventure...* corrupt in text, poetically inconsiderable, and... unlike Shakespeare'. This opinion has been shared by most, if not all, critics, with the result that general readers have been led to ignore it. This is a pity, because its subject, a girl's lament over a beautiful young man who has betrayed her, is of considerable interest in view of the subject-matter of most of the sonnets. The poem seems certainly to be by Shakespeare, and has seemed to some readers to qualify as one of the more neglected poems of its age. Its psychological interest is beyond dispute.

4

Nothing was now heard of the *Sonnets* until John Benson's pirated edition of 1640. It must be remembered, in connection with this, that in Shakespeare's time there was no such thing as author's copyright. Once a work had been registered, by fair means or foul, its copyright resided in the publisher. Close examination of Benson's edition reveals that it was in fact printed from Q; but the editor went to great lengths to conceal his theft. He misleadingly called it 'Poems by Wil. Shakespeare', and included in it one hundred and forty-six of the Q sonnets, *A Lovers Complaint*, the whole of the 1612 edition of *The Passionate Pilgrim, The Phoenix and the Turtle* and various poems by other writers, known and unknown – including elegies, by Milton and others, on Shakespeare's death. The contents he deliberately jumbled up, usually running two or three sonnets together as though they formed a single poem; for each of these concoctions he invented a fanciful title, such as 'A bashfull Lover', 'A dutifull Message', and so on. Significantly, he made some verbal changes: to make sonnets addressed to a man read as though addressed to a woman.

That Benson's edition was a consciously crooked undertaking is further revealed by his preface. He wrote: 'they [the contents of his volume] had not the fortune by reason of their Infancie in his death, to have the due accommodation of proportionable glory... I have been somewhat solicitus to bring this forth to the perfect view of all men...' In other words, although Benson had printed from Q, he pretends that it never existed.

The 1640 edition is, then, textually valueless. But two suggestive facts give it a greater importance than it deserves. First, that Benson was able to get away with it – even to the extent of tricking the Stationers' Company. He would not have dared to try this with *Venus and Adonis* or *The Rape of Lucrece*, because these, in 1640, were still popular and well-known poems. It seems likely that the *Sonnets* would have shared this popularity, or some of it, had the 1609 edition been available. It is significant that Thorpe, who did not entirely cease publishing activities until 1624, never re-issued them. Why not, unless the edition had been bought up, withdrawn, or otherwise suppressed? Secondly, Benson wrote in his preface that these 'sweetly composed Poems... in themselves appeare in the same purity, the Authour himselfe then living avouched...' Now Benson does not emerge as a reliable person, or as one much concerned with truth, so his word that Shakespeare had at sometime avouched the 'purity' of the *Sonnets* is worth little. What is more pertinent is that he should have felt impelled to say this at all. In the light of his alterations of gender in the text, it suggests that the *Sonnets* had had a bad reputation among some people – whether read or unread. Had Q originally been withdrawn, and passed quickly into a desired obscurity, then a few copies would have survived; one of these could easily have found its way into Benson's hands. By 1640 it would perhaps have been even less safe than in 1609 to publish a series of dubious love-poems. But Shakespeare was popular; the ownership of copyright in any of his works meant financial profit. Why not resurrect the unknown *Sonnets*, then, 'clean them up', and present them as hitherto unpublished?

5

Scholars cannot agree on whether Q is a bad, indifferent or good text. The most sensible view is that of H. E. Rollins, who writes in his monumental and invaluable *New Variorum* edition of the *Sonnets* (1944): 'In short, Q is an early seventeenth-century book printed in normal early seventeenth-century style.' Many of the 'errors' noted by Sir Sidney Lee, for example, who thought of Q as an unusually corrupt text, are discrepancies in spelling normal in the early seventeenth century. The use of italic is usually explainable in terms of the text. As George Wyndham, whose 1898 edition did much towards restoring the original, pointed out, only two capitalized words are not 'susceptible of rational explanation'. The text of Q is more fully discussed, however, particularly the punctuation, in the final section of this Introduction.

The first edition of the *Sonnets* not based on Benson's collection was issued by Bernard Lintott in 1711, and was fairly carefully edited by an unknown hand; but Benson's malign influence continued to be felt until, as Robins says, Edmond Malone's first edition (1780) gave it 'a *coup de grâce* among scholars'.

Modern readers of the *Sonnets* owe much to Edmond Malone. His was the first scholarly edition, and his annotations are still valuable. Unfortunately, however, Malone edited, emended and modernized according to the standards of poetic diction prevalent in his own not very critically enlightened times. The result is not altogether Shakespeare. Malone's re-punctuation, followed more or less by all modernizing editors, ignores both poetic subtlety and rhythmic function. The distortion of meaning is never great, but the elimination of difficulties and ambiguities that are an inherent part of the text results in impoverishment of the poetry.

The tendency of the present century, beginning with George Wyndham's edition of 1898, has been to return more closely to the original text – but not to the original punctuation. The fullest and most informative commentary is that of C. Knox Pooler in his Arden Edition of 1918, which is, however, marred by excessive conservatism and prudery. G. B. Harrison's Penguin edition of 1938 is reasonably close to Q, but is oddly inconsistent. In 1944 Hyder Edward Rollins published his *New Variorum* Edition, an invaluable summary of all the work, textual and critical, done on the *Sonnets* to that date. Apart from this, and the various facsimiles of Q, there has been no old-spelling edition; and this is the first critical one. Most modern critics prefer to quote from Q.

6

Arguments about when the *Sonnets* were written tend to be dominated by biographical theories. But as there is no conclusive evidence as to the identity of the young man addressed (the main theories are summarized in a later section), it is frivolous to try to date them by this means. Most sonnet-commentators have fallen into the error of applying their own biographical interpretation (for which there is necessarily no evidence, only supposition), and arguing for a date that fits it. It is wiser to be guided by the internal evidence provided by the text itself. Beyond the fact that all the *Sonnets* were written by 1609, and that two of them had been written by 1599, there is no concrete external evidence.

Furthermore, although all the probabilities are against it, the *Sonnets* may have been written spasmodically over a period of years. Alternatively, they could all have been written within a space of a few months. The fact that Shakespeare says, in 104, that he has known the Friend (as, for convenience and brevity, I shall call him) for three years does not prove that he had been writing sonnets to him for three years. Shakespeare's allusions to separations between the Friend and himself may refer to periods of anything from a few days to a matter of months or even years.

It is interesting that the internal evidence agrees with the 'average' date of composition, as calculated by Rollins from a compilation of all the conjectured dates. This indicates that Shakespeare began the sequence in mid-1593 and finished it in June 1599.

Samuel Butler's conjectured date of 1585-88, with which Dr Leslie Hotson agrees,* is unlikely. It is difficult to imagine that the Shakespeare of *Richard III* (1592-93) was capable of writing the *Sonnets;* the majority seem more natural to the Shakespeare of *Julius Caesar* (1599-1600) or *Hamlet* (1600-01). It is not generally supposed that many of them were written after about 1603; but the suggestion that they were is perhaps more difficult to refute on purely internal evidence than are the suggestions for the earlier dates, up to about 1595. The *Sonnets* display more poetic authority and show signs of greater maturity than either of Shakespeare's long narrative poems, *Venus.and Adonis* (1593) and *Lucrece* (1594). Their psychological preoccupations are indisputably closer to those found in *Henry IV* (1597-98), *Hamlet, Measure for Measure* and perhaps *All's Well That Ends Well* (1602-03) than in any other of the plays; but an anticipation of later themes is more likely to be found in what were probably 'private' poems than vice versa. The Shakespeare of *King Lear* (1605-06), on the other hand, seems beyond the *Sonnets.* A date of 1595-99 is open to the fewest objections. If the order of the sonnets in Q represents roughly the order in which Shakespeare wrote them, and there is every reason

**Shakespeare's Sonnets Dated.*

to suppose it does, none to suppose it doesn't, then he had completed 144 by 1599. *The Phoenix and the Turtle* (1601) would have made an appropriate conclusion to the 1609 edition: there is nothing in Shakespeare closer to the *Sonnets* as a whole, and to the tautness and apparent obscurity of many of them, than this poem.

Supposed 'parallels', in thought and imagery, some of which (though fewer than have been supposed) undoubtedly exist, do not help to fix a date, since it is impossible to tell which came first.

Scarcely more satisfactory are the attempts to date certain individual sonnets, since there is agreement on none of them. The only really important sonnet from this point of view is 107, where it is quite obvious that some specific and dateable event is referred to. Borrowings from other poets, if they could be established as borrowings and not sources, would set a date before which certain sonnets could not have been written; unfortunately for Lee and other commentators, not one of these alleged borrowings from contemporaries can be described as certain, or cannot be explained in some other way.

Sonnet 107, however, is a different matter. Lines 5-10:

> The mortall Moone hath her eclipse indur'de,
> And the sad Augurs mock their owne presage,
> Incertenties now crowne them-selves assur'de,
> And peace proclaimes Olives of endlesse age.
> Now with the drops of this most balmie time,
> My love...

obviously refer to something specific. Various theories have been advanced as to what this is, with dates ranging from 1579 to 1609. Most of these need not be taken seriously, but four are plausible and must be given full consideration.

Butler asserted that the defeat of the Armada in 1588 was referred to, concluding that 'the mortall Moone' was Queen Elizabeth, who 'had passed from under the shadow with undiminished brightness'. Dr Leslie Hotson, writing in 1949, without mentioning Butler, came to the same conclusion, but for different reasons: 'the mortall

Moone', he believes, refers to the shape of the attacking Spanish fleet, and he adduces some evidence, both written and pictorial, to show that this would have been fully understood by Shakespeare's readers. It is difficult, however, to accept 'indur'de' as meaning anything but 'passed through successfully'; and 'mortall', in this interpretation, has to mean 'deadly'.

G. B. Harrison, writing in 1928, advanced the theory that the line 'The mortall Moone hath her eclipse indur'de' refers to the Queen's recovery from serious illness in 1596, the year of her Grand Climacteric. He later added that the language was 'astrological', and that the danger to the Queen would also have been regarded as astrological (the sixty-third year, the Grand Climacteric, of a person's life was, from the popular contemporary astrological point of view, the most dangerous period, since it combines the numbers 7 and 9). Harrison adduced convincing evidence to show the likelihood of these 'astrological' threats to the Queen's life having been taken seriously by a large number of people, and his explanation is perhaps the most likely that has so far been advanced. On the other hand, possibly a reference only to a serious illness of the Queen was being made, and not to her Grand Climacteric; in this case, as Chambers has pointed out in rebuttal of Harrison, 1599 is just as likely a year as 1596: there were widespread rumours of her death in that year. Harrison pointed to the celebration of the success of the English fleet at Cadiz on 8 August 1596, as an explanation of lines 7-9; Chambers to the negotiations for a peace with Spain between 1599 and 1600. (But rumours of peace are as frequent as they are transitory. The tone of these lines does suggest a celebration of a victory as well as a hoped-for peace.)

There are serious objections to the theory, first advanced by Lee in 1898, that 107 refers to Queen Elizabeth's death – and also to James I's accession and Southampton's release from prison. First, 'the mortall Moone' and few, other than Hotson, have denied that this is a likely reference to the Queen, whose identification with the moon would have been familiar to anyone who could read – is said to have 'indur'de' its eclipse. How can this mean her death? It is unlikely that Shakespeare would have greeted the accession of the pitiable padded James I with the strongly-felt lines 'incertenties now crowne them-selves assur'de'. The line 'And the sad Augurs mock their owne presage' would not have been at all appropriate if 'mortall Moone' were merely an abstract symbol for the Crown, passing from the dead Elizabeth to the living James: it conjures up a picture of the prophets of disaster (amongst them, no doubt, the dismal and 'learned' astrologers themselves), whose very existence now mocks at their own forecasts. Pooler ingeniously suggests that the 'Augurs' were 'solemn politicians', and that their prophecy was not the correct one that the Queen would die, but the incorrect one that her death would be followed by war; but besides being far-fetched, this still fails to account for the 'Moone' having 'indur'de' her eclipse.

Meres's affirmation in 1598 of the existence of a number of sonnets by Shakespeare, in conjunction with the known publication of two of those coming late in the Q series in the following year, does constitute a strong supposition that a good deal of Q, or versions of it, had been completed by that time. On the other hand, internal evidence is very strong indeed against a period of composition beginning earlier than 1594.

It is significant that only biographical preconceptions, or in some instances a perverse desire to fill in Shakespeare's 'missing years', have led commentators and writers on the *Sonnets* to dispute this seriously; and, as will be seen, the most likely biographical theory is no more than a guess.

7

The number of ways in which one hundred and fifty-four poems may be arranged is astronomical. Changes have been made on both biographical and aesthetic grounds, and have shown varying respect for the original order; most are not even worthy of consideration. Butler* shifted only a few sonnets, so that their position should do justice to his biographical theory. Brooke (ed. 1936)*, on the other

* For these and other references see *Select Biography*), p118.

hand, based his more drastic re-arrangement on the supposition that the sonnets had originally been composed in batches of from two to five, on single sheets of paper; the dislocation of these sheets, he claimed, is responsible for the alleged incorrectness of the Q order. Innumerable other schemes have been propounded, most of them dictated by notions less likely than those of Butler and Brooke, none of them by demonstrable facts.

Only one scheme, that of Sir Denys Bray (1925, revised 1938), attempted to determine the order by a purely mechanical criterion. Bray claimed that his was the first arrangement to have been formulated on the basis of 'hard fact': certain sonnets, he asserted, were 'linked' to one another by the repetition of words and rhymes. These might occur in any line. On this loose principle he sorted out the sonnets into nine groups, each group being determined by 'rhyme-link'. His re-arrangement of the sonnets in each group, however, was no less subjective than any other. He did scant service to his cause by proclaiming a new order in 1938. The weakness of his scheme, apart from the unconvincing nature of the 'rhyme-link' itself, is that the number of arrangements that may be evolved from it is almost infinite. And, as Chambers wrote, the 'quarrel with Sir Denys really rests, not so much upon what he has done, as on what he has undone... he has rent asunder many sense-links... which are clearly apparent in Thorpe's text'.

Nowadays we dismiss Benson's re-arrangement as having been dictated by the most vulgar of motives; but even the more sensible of modern schemes, such as Butler's or Brooke's or Bray's, have little more to justify them in the face of the perfectly coherent order of 1609. After all, Benson did have a commercial reason: he was a crooked publisher, pretending that the text had never before existed. Thorpe's order may not represent the exact order in which Shakespeare wrote the *Sonnets:* poets as frequently anticipate themselves as they regress. But there is little doubt that 1-126, in Q, represent Shakespeare's arrangement. Objections to this order, which can always be concocted on one ground or another, arise more from a desire to change it than from any difficulties inherent in it. Its perfect psychological sense, as a sequence, is its most self-evident feature.

The 'Mistress' sequence (127-152) is admittedly separate, and there is no reason to suppose that this was not written contemporaneously with 1-126, and perhaps at the same time as 40-42. It would have been confusing to mix sonnets written to the Friend with ones written to the Mistress.

Some critics have of course contended that many of 1-126 (notably 78-80) concern not the Friend but the Mistress; but this not only introduces an entirely unnecessary complication, but also has nothing to commend it. It is unreasonable to attempt changes when a perfectly intelligible order is one of the few relatively certain features that Q can offer, and the weight of its authenticity in this matter must be accounted greater than that of any editorial theories of a later date.

8

It is mainly from the dedication-page of Q that inferences as to the identity of the Friend have been drawn. According to Butler, 'Mr W.H.' must have signified the Friend's initials because, by the word 'begetter', Thorpe must have meant, not 'procurer', but 'inspirer'. 'Admitting the title-page as correct,' he wrote, ' "onlie Begetter" would have been taken to mean that though Shakespeare's brain was the womb wherein the sonnets grew, the influence which had fecundated that brain had proceeded solely from Mr W.H.' This is by no means as obvious as Butler would have liked: whether Thorpe meant 'inspirer' or not, he seems almost certainly to have meant 'procurer' as well. The dedication of a publisher is more likely to express gratitude for provision of profitable copy than for the rather more obscure honour of having inspired it. Butler's insistence on this point is explained by his belief that the Friend's name was William Hews. This idea had been put forward before, but less dogmatically, on the grounds that the line 'A man in hew all *Hews* in his controwling' (20) contains a play on the name of the person to whom the sonnet was addressed. (However, this may equally well be some private joke: a reference to a third person called Hews – someone who was dependent on the Friend, or followed him about, or owed him money.) But Butler was on surer ground in describing Lee's attempts to show that the 'Will' sonnets (135, 136, 143) contain no play on the name of the Friend as 'inconclusive'. He thereupon began to search the records for a possible William Hews, eventually finding one who might fill his bill. This was a navy man who, having been a steward for 'many years', was appointed as a ship's cook in 1633-34, and died in 1636-37. The language of 26 alone makes a person of such low social status unlikely, and this theory is clearly very flimsy. No date of birth of this William Hews or Hughes (it is variously spelt) is available; and surely, if indeed the Friend was not of high rank, then he is more likely to have been an actor, or at least a literary hanger-on, than a ship's steward.

Another Hews was propounded by Lord Alfred Douglas. In his book *The True History of Shakespeare's Sonnets* (1933) he had endorsed Butler's view that the Friend was called William Hews, but had stated his preference for Oscar Wilde's theory of an actor of that name. Wilde had put forward this view in 1889 in *The Portrait of Mr W.H.*, but without any evidence to support it. In 1938 in *The Times Literary Supplement* Douglas announced his discovery of a William Hewes who had been admitted to the freedom of Canterbury in 1593, after having served as an apprentice to Christopher Marlowe's shoemaker father, John. Douglas suggested that Christopher had taken Hewes up to London 'to perform female parts'; unfortunately, his promise of further details remained unfulfilled at the time of his death in 1945.

The wretched Lee, who cannot be said to have had any fixed theory, since he changed his ground from year to year with disconcerting suddenness, at one time proposed that Mr W.H. was a pirate printer, William Hall, who had procured the copy (not inspired it) for Thorpe, and who was in league with him for the purpose of obtaining likely MSS. Some people have believed that 'Mr W. H. All' was a mistake for 'MR W. HALL', though Lee held no brief for this.

The identification of the Friend with Henry Wriothesley, third Earl of Southampton (1573-1624), although it was not proposed until comparatively late (1817) in the history of Sonnet controversy, has met with a popular acceptance out of proportion to its intrinsic merits.

Southampton was undoubtedly at one time Shakespeare's literary patron: *Venus* and *Lucrece* are both dedicated to him. Seizing on this, 'Southamptonites' point out that in 78 Shakespeare addresses the Friend as his patron. Now while this sonnet does unequivocally state that other poets had written poems addressed to (or perhaps under the patronage of) the Friend (thus incidentally doing serious harm to Butler's sea-cook theory), it does not necessarily address him as Shakespeare's *patron*. It merely states that Shakespeare has written about him. We must accept, on the evidence of 78, that the Friend either *was* a literary patron of some distinction, or that his beauty and influence inspired many poets to write about him. The latter theory presupposes, of course, that there was a coterie of poets all of whom were at odds with one another in order to gain his favours. If the former theory be preferred, then it would appear that Southampton – the ready-made patron of Shakespeare – is after all a likely candidate for the Friend. But apart from his admitted patronage of Shakespeare in 1594, Southampton's claims are less well-founded than those of another nobleman, also a patron of poets, William Herbert, Earl of Pembroke (1580-1630). Pembroke had been advanced in this connection by James Boaden in 1832, only fifteen years after Dr Nathan Drake had first put forward Southampton.

Beside the language of 78 and the fact of Southampton's patronage of Shakespeare, all that Drake could adduce in support of his theory was that Southampton may, when his proposed marriage to Elizabeth Vernon met with bitter opposition from the Queen, have declared that 'if he could not marry the object of his choice, he would die single'; and 26, he contended, duplicates the *Lucrece* dedication. The first of these reasons is plainly absurd; and the second means nothing: if 26 does resemble the dedication of *Lucrece*, this tells us no more than that poets sometimes use the same sort of language on different occasions. 'Southamptonites', who favour an early date of composition, can in fact point to a simpler explanation than Drake's: in November 1594 Southampton paid out, £5,000 in order to be released from his apparently unwilling promise to marry Lady Elizabeth Vere, whose grandfather, Lord Burghley, had enthusiastically urged the match, to which the Earl had always been bitterly opposed.

Nothing of importance has been offered in support of this theory since Drake. It gained such wide currency largely because Lee, who was for many years considered an authority on Shakespeare, even by discerning people, inexplicably and silently adopted it in 1897; his re-statement of the case, however, added nothing positive to it.

William Herbert's liaison with Mary Fitton, a Maid of Honour at court, who had a son by him in 1601, as well as his reputation for sensuality, suggests that he was not above the sort of behaviour that Shakespeare attributes to the Friend. Both in 1595 and 1598 he bitterly opposed plans to marry him off; and as a result of his refusal to marry the mother of his child in 1601 he was, for a short time, imprisoned by the Queen. (He did not marry until 1604.) The First Folio Shakespeare of 1623 was dedicated to Pembroke and his brother Philip by the publishers, Heminge and Condell, who had of course known Shakespeare intimately, in these terms: 'But since your L.L. have beene pleas'd to thinke these trifles some-thing, heretofore: and have prosequuted both them, and their Authour living, with so much favour: we hope... you will use the like indulgence toward them, you have done to their parent.' This at least disposes of Lee's assertion, made after he had abandoned the Pembroke theory, that there was 'no evidence' that Shakespeare had ever known Pembroke.

Chambers's suggestion, in *Shakespearean Gleanings* (1944), that Shakespeare may have been hired by Sir George Carey 'to stimulate the imagination of young Herbert' and to dispel his reluctance to marry his daughter Elizabeth in 1595, is not an unlikely one. Sir

George was the son of Lord Hunsdon, of whose company of players Shakespeare was then a leading member. Chambers further believes, with good reason, that Shakespeare had been a member of the Earl of Pembroke's company before this. If so, he would have had opportunities to meet his son. It was previously believed that Pembroke was not in London before 1598; but Rollins has shown that he was at Court in the October and November of 1595.

Even Butler's objection to Pembroke on the grounds that an Earl would never have been addressed as 'Mr' may be met: Mr W. H.'s initials, if he were merely the procurer, may have been the only point of resemblance between him and the Earl; Thorpe may have been pulling wool over the eyes of his readers quite deliberately, both as policy and as a joke. Ben Jonson, in dedicating his *Epigrams* to Pembroke in 1616, remarked: 'My Lord *While you cannot change your merit, I dare not change your title... For, when I made them, I had nothing in my conscience, to expressing of which I did need a cipher*': he may have been alluding to Thorpe's 'disguised' dedication. His words certainly require some explanation. In the course of the same dedication he says also, *'my* Epigrammes, *which, though they tarry danger in the sound, doe not therefore seek your shelter.'* If Jonson were referring to Thorpe, then it would seem as though the name 'Shakespeare's Sonnets' had carried 'danger in the sound': that is, that they had been the subject of scandalous gossip.

In 1613 the poet George Wither had inscribed his *Abuses Stript, and Whipt*: 'To himselfe, G. W. wisheth *all happinesse'*. This certainly looks like a parody of the Q dedication. Gerald Massey suggested in 1872 that 'Ben Jonson... points out William Herbert as the object of [Thorpe's inscriptions]... [Jonson's dedication] looks like a reply to [Wither's], as though it were an endeavour to saddle Thorpe with the responsibility of publishing Shakespeare's Sonnets and dedicating them to the Earl.'*

In 1860 a German critic, D. Barnstorff, casually threw out a theory

*It is interesting that Pembroke himself published a book of verse, some of it very obscene, in which there are poems to a 'dark lady'.

about 'Mr W. H.' which is lent some support by Wither's dedication 'to himselfe'. This was that 'W. H.' stands for 'William Himself'. Barnstorff's innocent suggestion, put forward without elaboration, is at least as worthy as anybody else's guess; but it was ridiculed in its time, and now seems to have been forgotten. Thorpe was certainly capable of making a joke of this kind; he had displayed an odd sense of humour in others of his dedications, including one to Pembroke himself.

Many other identifications of the Friend have of course been made. They range from wild guesses such as William Hathaway, Shakespeare's brother-in-law, to the 'brothers' Southampton and Pembroke. But none, including those of Southampton and Pembroke, is more than a guess.

All this belongs to the realm of biographical conjecture; while it has played a large part in the history of Sonnet controversy, it must not lead us, as C. S. Lewis has reminded us, to treat the *Sonnets* as a novel or an autobiography. It is neither safe nor fruitful to draw conclusions about their poetic meaning from such conjecture. The poetry itself tells us, in Lewis's words, that Shakespeare's feeling for the Friend was 'too lover-like for that of ordinary male friendship... yet... this does not seem to be the poetry of full-blown pederasty'. Knowing the identity of the man who inspired these poems is not going to solve the problem of their meaning.

9

Attempted identifications of the Mistress (40-42, 127-152) have proved more tenuous even than those of the Friend. There is really nothing in the *Sonnets* that can be described as evidence of her status in society; only of her character. Any woman, from a high-class courtesan to a Lady-in-Waiting or a Duchess, might have possessed such characteristics. Guesses at her identity vary from mere fancies, such as Queen Elizabeth, to more plausible suggestions (usually prompted by preconceptions about the Friend), such as Mary Fitton, the Maid of Honour who was Pembroke's mistress. Harrison, with a surprising dogmatism, asserted in 1933 that the Mistress was a negro prostitute, probably a certain Lucy Negro, Abbess de Clerkenwell. This is not impossible, despite Rollins's scorn, but it is of course no more than a supposition.

A more intriguing problem raised by the Mistress, in the absence of any real clues as to her identity, is that of the exact significance of Shakespeare's references to her 'colour'. Whether it can altogether be explained by the known fact that 'blacke was not counted faire' is open to doubt. One of the reasons for the vogue of fairness in Shakespeare's time was of course that the Queen was blonde. There is obviously a good deal of verbal and 'symbolic' significance in Shakespeare's obsession with the Mistress's dark colouring (see Commentary), but it does seem possible that this was occasioned by some marked physical oddity in her. It is not difficult to imagine that a negress – a rarity in the London of Shakespeare's time – would have attracted a body of 'admirers', consisting of men both of literary and social position. Nor is it unlikely that in this event some kind of 'mystique' might have been built up around her. The semi-casual, fashionable pursuit of a woman on account of her novel colour, by a number of his contemporaries, would explain some of Shakespeare's more cryptic utterances about her appearance, such as the opening lines of 127. There is a tone, here, of scorn for what is described as a new way of looking at beauty; but it seems as though the reference were private rather than general. Shakespeare felt that he understood and saw through the Mistress, while others paid suit to her for the wrong reasons and were taken in by her. They may be the 'nimble Jackes' of 128 (see Commentary).

10

Eight of the sonnets (78-86, with the exception of 81) are concerned with other poets, and apparently with one poet in particular, who had been writing in praise of, or had been inspired by, the Friend. In 78 Shakespeare complains that 'every *Alien* pen hath got my use'; likewise in 82 he refers to 'their grosse painting';

in 85 'other write good wordes'. In 79, 80, 83, 84 and 86, however, only one poet is referred to (if Shakespeare is accepted as one of 'both your Poets' in 83). Conjectures about the identity of this poet, who is known as the 'Rival', have been many. The most popular candidate is George Chapman; others who have been put forward include Marlowe, Daniel, Drayton, Spenser and Sidney.

Of these poets the first line of 86, 'the proud full saile of his great verse', if it is taken at its face-value, could apply only to Marlowe, Chapman or possibly Spenser. Marlowe, however, was murdered in 1593, and is really too early for serious consideration; nor is there anything to suggest that he wrote any poems, now lost, in praise of a man, though it is clear that he had homosexual feelings. The few advocates of Spenser point out, with some justice, that Shakespeare might well have accorded him such high praise, both on account of his reputation and his merits; nothing else, however, points towards him, and he is generally unlikely. Chapman, on the other hand, had continued Marlowe's *Hero and Leander* (this was first published in 1598, but Shakespeare could of course have read it in MS well before that time), and in doing so had excelled himself. Shakespeare, as the author of *Venus* and *Lucrece,* might well have felt both admiration for and envy of Chapman on account of this achievement; it is a better poem, and Shakespeare would have recognized this. It is not suggested, of course, that Chapman's *Hero* (which was dedicated to Lady Walsingham) had anything to do with the Friend; the point is that it would explain the admiration which Shakespeare clearly demonstrates in 86.

It is often contended, however, that the whole of this sonnet, including the first line, is both ironic and bitterly sarcastic; but this seems to me to constitute a grave misreading. The whole point is that Shakespeare's 'line' is 'infeebled' because the 'matter' (of the Friend's beauty) has been *successfully* taken from him by the Rival. If you admit that X is superb at the pole-vault, but assert that the reason you did not enter the event was, not his excellence, but the fact that he stole your pole, you are by no means, after all, therefore implying that you had been sarcastic in your admission of his ability

– even if you cannot help thinking of him as a thief.) Besides, no one can seriously suggest that 80, in which Shakespeare calls the Rival a 'better spirit' and refers to 'my sawsie barke (inferior farre to his)', is ironic. True, it has been explained away as the product of another mood, typical of the Elizabethans-exaggerated humility; however, it is not demonstrably typical of Shakespeare, who would have been speaking only the plain truth had he been thinking of himself as the poet of *Venus* and *Lucrece,* and of Chapman as the poet of *Hero.* There is a kind of profound criticism implied in the phrase 'gulls him with intelligence' (see Commentary), as from one poet to another; but to discern 'amused contempt' in it, as one writer has done, is to call the whole of 80, and the first line of 86, both insincere and petulant.

It is reasonably certain that since 1594 there had been rivalry between the two poets. Robert Greene, probably addressing Nashe, had in his posthumous *Groatsworth of Wit* (1592) savagely attacked Shakespeare as a mere actor. Now although Chapman was probably no more a University man than Shakespeare, he associated with University men and he was more learned than most of them; and, as we know from his own frequent and often boring references to the subject, as a poet he set much store upon learning. Some of Greene's original animosity against Shakespeare as a *Johannes Factotum,* an ignorant upstart, may well have passed to Chapman and his 'cryptic' group by 1594. Furthermore, as the late J. A. K. Thomson pointed out in his interesting book *Shakespeare and the Classics,* Chapman himself may have had an added reason in 1594 to dislike Shakespeare. In this year *Venus and Adonis* was published: he may well have envied the popular success that was probably achieved by this poem, which, by his somewhat involute standards, would have seemed both superficial and even anti-poetic. Being based on a classical theme, it would have represented itself to him as a travesty of all that poetry ought to be. There are almost certainly angry references to it in his obscure *Shadow of Night* (1594), a poem spoiled by its over-involved theme, but nevertheless seriously underrated by scholars. Shakespeare, meanwhile, may have lampooned

Chapman and his theories in the character of Holofernes in *Love's Labour's Lost*, probably written during 1594-95.

However, Chapman (if not some of the other members of his coterie) rose above his theories, and it is not stretching matters too far to see in 78-86 Shakespeare's generous recognition of this. There is every reason to suppose, also, that Shakespeare, as one with 'small Latin and less Greek' would have been impressed, and rightly so, by Chapman's translation of Homer, which, even if a Latin crib was employed, certainly outdid Shakespeare in classical scholarship. The first part of this was not published until 1598, but copies of it were probably in circulation before then. This brings us to the most striking evidence, first put forward by Thomson, for Chapman as the 'Rival'. In the *Inductio* (dedicated to Prince Henry) to *The Teares of Peace* (1609), Chapman describes how he came to be directly inspired by the spirit of Homer:

> '...I, invisibly, went prompting thee
> To those faire greens where thou didst English me.'
> Scarce had he uttered this, when well I knew
> It was my Prince's Homer...

Chapman states in the course of the *Inductio* that this happened 'on the hill Next Hitchin's left hand', and since he probably left the place of his birth, which was near Hitchin, in 1570, it is clear that it was an experience of his early years. It represents, of course, a claim that he had been 'by spirits taught to write'; such a bold claim as this would have been common knowledge many years before Chapman put it on official record. At the conclusion of the same poem Chapman seems to echo Shakespeare:

> The heavy body of my humble Muse;
> That thy great Homer's spirit in her may use
> Her topless flight, and bear thy fame above
> The reach of mortals and their earthly love...

Thomson thinks that Shakespeare was laughing at Chapman's absurd claim; but the quality of Chapman's poetry at its best, and the tone of 86, belie this interpretation. There is no reason to suppose that Shakespeare would have wholly laughed at Chapman's idea of poetry, as he expressed it (echoing Horace) in a dedication to Matthew Roydon (1598): 'The profane multitude I hate, and only consecrate my strange poems to those searching spirits, whom learning hath made noble...' There was a sense, and I think he expresses this in some of the 'Rival' sonnets, in which, as a popular playwright, Shakespeare envied and admired it. It is not likely that at this time (1595-1600) he put a very high poetic value on his own plays – the value we put upon them should not mislead us on this point.

11

A summary of Sonnet speculations would not be complete without a mention of *Willobie His Avisa*. This poem of seventy-two cantos, purporting to be 'The True Picture of a Modest Maid, and of a chast and constant wife', was first published by John Windet in 1594. It was reprinted at least three, probably four times, the last edition being issued in 1635 by William Stansby, who had bought the rights from Windet. The poem owed its popularity to its ostensible subject; but in 1599 it was listed in the Stationers' Register as one of three books to be called in, and from this and from other curious circumstances surrounding it, it may be inferred that it was almost certainly, in Lewis's words, 'a scandalous *roman à clef*. Unfortunately the key or keys to its mysteries are now beyond recovery.

The poem was introduced to the public by one 'Hadrian Dorrell', who claimed to have found it amongst the papers of his friend, 'Henry Willobie', 'departed for foreign lands', and of whose existence there is some very reasonable doubt. It deals with the successful efforts of a woman, Avisa (*A*mans *u*xor *i*nviolate *s*emper *a*manda), to resist attacks on her virtue by various determined gentlemen ('Ruffians, Roysters, young Gentlemen, and lustie

Captaines, which all shee quickly cuts off'), including 'Cavaleiro', 'D. B. A French man', 'Dydimus Harco, Anglo-Germanicus', and finally 'Henrico Willobego, Italo Hispanensis' himself. It is a highly amusing and literate poem, obviously full of private jokes and allusions, and equally obviously more than tongue-in-cheek about its main theme, to which, however, it owed its popular life of about forty or fifty years.

There is a passing reference to Shakespeare in some prefatory verses, in the same stanza-form as the poem itself: *In Praise of Willobie his Avisa*, signed Vigilantius Dormitanus:

> Yet *Tarquyne plucks* his glistering grape,
> And *Shake-speare,* paints poor *Lucrece* rape.

But the section of *Willobie* which has attracted the attention of Sonnet commentators is that dealing with the attempted seduction of Avisa by 'H. W.', Willobie himself. H. W., unable to bear any longer his 'secret grief', asks the advice of his friend 'W. S.', 'who not long before had tryed the curtesy of the like passion. W. S., however, instead of 'stopping the issue', 'took pleasure for a tyme to see him bleed... miserable comforter comforting his friend with an impossibilitie... he determined to see whether it would sort to a happier end for this new actor, than it did for the old player.' W. S. gives H. W. some cynical advice about how to win women; but the latter is of course unsuccessful.

Many writers have linked 'W. S.' with Shakespeare, and it is true that there is no other who will fit so well. But it is a far cry from this to 'establishing' that in Avisa, alias Mistress Davenant, we have the 'Dark Lady' and in 'H. W.' the Friend of the Sonnets. No serious evidence has been adduced to prove any of this.

G. B. Harrison, in an essay following his reprint of *Willobie* (1926), explained the poem as a ripost of the so-called 'School of Night' against Essex, Southampton and *Lucrece*, and ascribed the authorship to Matthew Roydon. The existence of this group, consisting of Ralegh, Chapman, Roydon, Herriot, Edwardes and others, has been questioned, but not very cogently, and Harrison's solution of the problem is the most convincing. Miss M.C. Bradbrook, in *The School of Night* (1936), agreed with Harrison but thought, wisely, that *Willobie* was the result of composite authorship.

The solutions to the problems set by this obscure satire, if they could ever be obtained, would probably contain some matters valuable to the biography of Shakespeare. It is unlikely that they could throw much light on the *Sonnets*.

12

The first known person to discern signs of a not altogether 'respectable' autobiographical situation behind the *Sonnets* was evidently John Benson. Whether he knew anything specific about the relationships that inspired them is problematical; but if he did have certain knowledge, it would have made him all the more determined to remove all 'scandalous' elements from his edition. As I have pointed out, the fact that Benson was able to hoodwink both the authorities and the public into thinking that his was the first edition very strongly suggests that Q had been withdrawn or suppressed. Thorpe, who, we may well guess, knew the 'inside story', no doubt hoped to profit by the very 'scandalous' nature of the publication that Benson seems to have been at pains to conceal. (It could well have been that in 1609 the words 'Shakespeare's Sonnets' awakened the same kind of vulgar curiosity in people, though on a smaller scale, as would be evinced today by the appearance of 'The Authentic Casement Diaries, printed for the first time'.

It was not until the latter half of the eighteenth century, however, that commentators began to give serious attention to the autobiographical element. The notion that the *Sonnets* are entirely fictional has persisted to this day. On the one hand there are the assertions of such critics as Schlegel (1796) that Shakespeare deliberately 'bared his soul'; on the other, the denial of the presence of any autobiographical element at all: they are 'dramatic' or 'literary exercises'. Lee, for example, having discovered to his own satisfaction that Elizabethan sonnets as a whole were both written to a convention and also extremely imitative of classical and Italian models, applied this general theory to Shakespeare's. His attempts to elucidate their 'sources', however, were as conspicuously unconvincing as his other criticism.

Both the extreme views avoid the real issue. All poetry has its roots in subjective experience. There is nothing, in one sense, that does not. Even if the *Sonnets* were 'literary exercises', they would reflect facets of Shakespeare's own experience. You cannot write poems about being in love with a man unless you have been in love with one; and if you have not, you would not wish to write about it. On the other hand, the notion that Shakespeare deliberately engaged himself in a planned autobiographical project is difficult to accept. It is not easy to discern any pattern or plan. The *Sonnets* seem to have been occasioned by day-to-day experience of an intense kind; and they seem to have been written from day to day and from week to week, without much thought, at any rate at the time they were written, of publication. Meres said that Shakespeare's sonnets were in circulation amongst his 'private friends', and if these are the sonnets he meant, then the phrase is significant: they were not, he plainly implied, intended for general circulation. His phrase allows of no other inference. But they are so extraordinary a literary production, so obviously of high poetic value, that most critics have found it impossible to think of them as not having been written to a plan, and with publication in mind. But it may well be that the sonnets are of a higher poetic value than Shakespeare's two ambitious narrative poems (and this is surely a universally accepted judgement) because they were not written with the public in mind. Indeed, the plays themselves, or most of them, are superior to these two poems (of which he certainly had higher hopes) for the same reason: the poetry of the plays was incidental to their main purpose, which was to entertain the public successfully and make their author some money.

This does not imply that Shakespeare did not care: he simply did best without being too much concerned with literary fashion and literary critics. Certainly the *Sonnets*, together with poems by Chapman, Ralegh and Donne, were among the most original non-dramatic productions of their time.

Shakespeare did not handle the sonnet-form, in purely technical terms, as elegantly as Sidney; but he chose it as a vehicle for something that was far more 'casual', in literary terms, far nearer reality, in poetic terms. When we read the *Sonnets*, we are reading something that Shakespeare, when he wrote them, possibly never intended for any public eye. The 'sincerity' of *Astrophel and Stella*, when placed beside the matter-of-factness of the *Sonnets*, is seen to be artificial.

While it is a waste of time to play the game of putting names to the people who figure in the *Sonnets*, it is a different matter together to infer a human situation from what they state.

But there are difficulties in the way of this. So penetrating a mind as Coleridge's found it necessary to hedge on the matter of the autobiographical element. He wrote, astonishingly: 'It seems to me that the sonnets could only come from a man deeply in love, and in love with a woman...' and (of all Shakespeare's work) he declared that there is 'not even an allusion to that very worst of all possible vices'. This general uneasiness about the moral propriety of the *Sonnets* is summed up in the words, quoted by Rollins, of Leon de Wailly, in 1834: 'Good heavens!... He instead of she? Can I be mistaken? Can these sonnets be addressed to a man? Shakespeare! Great Shakespeare!'

Strangely enough, in *The Portrait of Mr W. H.* (1888), Oscar Wilde specifically denied that there was anything 'unlawful' in Shakespeare's love for the Friend; it is significant that a few years afterwards a jury at the Old Bailey rejected similar protestations made on his own behalf.

It was not until Butler's edition of 1898 that Shakespeare's homosexuality was openly canvassed. Butler asserted that for a short time the relationship between the two men was 'more Greek than English'. 'Is it likely,' he asked, 'that there was ever afterwards a day in his life in which the remembrance of that "night of woe" did not at some time or another rise up before him and stab him? Nay, is it not quite likely that this great shock may in the end have brought him prematurely to the grave?' He based his conclusions on the belief that 'between sonnets 32 and 33... there has been a catastrophe'. 'Mr W. H. must have lured him on.' The key to this catastrophe Butler found in 34: 'The trap... I believe to have been a cruel and most disgusting practical joke... I cannot... doubt that Shakespeare was... made to "travel forth without" that "cloak" which, if he had not been lured, we may be sure that he would not have discarded. Hardly had he laid the cloak aside before he was surprised by a preconcerted scheme, and very probably roughly handled...'

If we must choose between this theory and the rebuke which it drew from Larbaud, who attacked Butler for believing 'that the Great National Poet was on the verge of having what is conveniently called bad morals! To suggest the word "pederasty" with reference to so pure a glory!', then we must choose Butler, even if he did make unwarranted assumptions.

A similar view to that held by Butler, though much modified, is found *in The Mutual Flame*, G. Wilson Knight's provocative and interesting study of *The Phoenix and the Turtle* and the *Sonnets*. Mr Knight's critical theory of poetry might be summed up as a kind of bi-sexual transcendentalism, and sometimes this leads him to overvalue or misinterpret his material; but his critical examination of the *Sonnets,* when he forgets his rather tiresome main thesis, is sensitive and valuable. It is significant that his discussion, in this light, is more convincing than that of Patrick Cruttwell in his essay *A Reading of Shakespeare's Sonnets*, first printed in the *Hudson Review,* and later included in his book *The Shakespearean Moment*. Cruttwell adheres to the theory that Shakespeare's feelings towards the Friend were not homosexual, but merely typical of Renaissance 'friendship'. He makes out as good a case as can be made out, but it remains unconvincing. For one thing, Shakespeare was never a conventional poet; for another, the tone of the *Sonnets* is altogether too personal and too intense for them to be regarded as 'conventional' in Cruttwell's sense.

The law itself on this question, which is surely relevant, was fairly explicit. Until 1533 buggery had been only an ecclesiastical crime, but in that year it was made a felony punishable by death. Probably this was because of the state of affairs exposed by the Dissolution of the Monasteries. The statute was subsequently repealed by Edward VI, but finally re-enacted in 1562; it remained a capital offence until 1828. However, few prominent persons seem to have been executed because of it. Nicholas Udall, author of *Ralph Roister Doister*, and headmaster of Eton, a known sadist and homosexual, was accused of connivance at theft and 'unnatural crime' in 1541, and pleaded guilty to the latter offence; but by 1553 he was again a headmaster, this time of Westminster. Bacon, who indulged in homosexual practices with his servants, was never even proceeded against on these grounds; but perhaps this was because James I was himself a notorious homosexual. In his son's reign the Earl of Castlehaven and his two servants were less lucky, and were executed (the charges against the Earl included sodomy on his own wife; but the two servants were indicted solely on homosexual charges). Clearly, then, Shakespeare might have come to feel in 1609 that the publication of these love-poems, most of them addressed to a man, placed him in some jeopardy. Even if he had consented to the publication (and there is no evidence that he did not) this may have been brought home to him by his friends; or if it was generally known to whom they were addressed, then this person may have had a hand in suppressing them or buying them up. It is unlikely that Shakespeare would have failed to remember that one of the charges outstanding against Marlowe at the time of his murder had been that he was alleged to have said 'all thei that love not tobacco and boyes are fooles'.

The fact that Shakespeare may have felt apprehension about the publication of the *Sonnets* does not in itself imply that there had actually been an 'illegal' association between himself and his friend. It does, however, very strongly suggest that, the *Sonnets* were an essentially personal and private composition; there is nothing else in Elizabethan literature in which a man so openly avows love for another man.

It is the nature of this love that poses the real human problem of the *Sonnets*. Shakespeare's physical feelings towards the so-called 'Dark Lady' are unequivocal, even if his attitude towards her is cryptic. His feelings towards the Friend are less easy to analyse. In 1-17 he urges him to marry, but more important than this, which is perhaps the most 'conventional' aspect of the whole sequence, is what he implies about the Friend's character.

There is every reason to suppose that 1-17 were written earlier than the rest; it is likely indeed that Shakespeare did begin ambitiously, with an idea of producing a sequence in the artificial manner of such contemporaries as Daniel and Sidney. This would account for the relatively impersonal or 'disengaged' tone of the first half-dozen or so, and for the exhortation to marry, comparatively formal and meaningless in itself. The passages that have been quoted (mostly by Lee) in an attempt to demonstrate that this 'urge to marry' was a 'commonplace' of Elizabethan literature are not very convincing: eight sonnets by Daniel urging his mistress to marry and so gain immortality, and the first twelve sonnets from Sidney's *Arcadia* are not enough to justify Lee's characteristic assertion that 'nothing was commoner'. But it existed; and the point is that the 'formal' tone is present: Shakespeare did not mean it as literally as he meant what he said in the later sonnets. By the time he came to write 20, he had already forgotten all about ambition or convention: there is nothing else like this in literature.

The key to what Shakespeare was fumbling towards when he spoke of marriage and procreation is found in 10:

> But that thou none lov'st is most evident:
> For thou art so possest with murdrous hate,
> That gainst thy self thou stickst not to conspire,...

This is not just a conceit, a way of saying that the Friend has *overlooked* the fact that he is damaging himself by failing to get married; it means that he is so narcissistic, so in love with himself, that he is in danger of being unable to love outside himself:

Or who is he so fond will be the tombe,
Of his self: love to stop posterity? (3)

and therefore never 'using' his rare beauty:

For having traffike with thy self: alone,
Thou of thy self: thy sweet selfe dost deceave,... (4)

The impression conveyed, and it is particularly explicit in 6, is that the Friend is so far consumed in self-love as to be too jealous to produce 'copies' of himself. The poetic emphasis in these opening sonnets is really laid upon this vanity. He is exhorted to give – to love; if he does not, then the world of death and time will deal with him – and they will do so because he has not deserved more:

No love toward others in that bosome sits
That on himselfe such murdrous shame commits. (9)

Marriage and procreation are the metaphors for the 'use' which a possessor of beauty must make of it if he is not to destroy it. In the final sonnet of this series (17), Shakespeare warns the Friend that if he does not procreate his kind (and this is only a way of exhorting him to love, to give himself away) then his beauty, as celebrated in Shakespeare's poems, will be 'scorn'd':

And your true rights be termd a Poets rage.

And he ends:

But were some childe of yours alive that time,
You should live twise in it, and in my rime.

In other words, if the Friend does not free himself from the meshes of his self-love, then his beauty will be destroyed: it will not be worthy of perpetuation in poetry, because poetry is concerned above all else with love, which is the prey of Time and Death.

But wherefore do not you a mightier waie
Make warre uppon this bloudie tirant time?
And fortifie your selfe in your decay
With meanes more blessed then my barren rime?
....
To give away your selfe, keeps your selfe still,
And you must live drawne by your owne sweet skill. (16)

It is difficult to understand why editors have disturbed the order of 1-20. They provide a clear record of how Shakespeare began to write sonnets urging a boy to marry, either because he was ambitious to produce a sequence on a suitably academic theme, or because he was asked to do so, or both; and how he then became interested enough in his subject to reproach him for his self-love, and how he finally fell in love with him. The tone of criticism becomes increasingly personal from 1 to 9, and then in 10 Shakespeare finally makes his appeal: 'for love of me'. By the time he came to write 20, there was no doubt in his own mind as to how he regarded the Friend.

A hitherto 'normal' person who undergoes a homosexual experience is faced with a peculiar and disconcerting problem. The person with whom he is in love is, so to speak, 'made in his own image': thus there is inevitably an element of self-love and of sexual vanity in his attitude. This element is present in every kind of love; but whereas heterosexual love has the power to transcend it, homosexual love cannot.

The *Sonnets*, then, provide a poetic insight into what may be described, paradoxically, as a heterosexual's homosexual experience. Shakespeare wanted to love the Friend without sex; the narcissistic element introduced into the situation was, to him, a wasting enemy, like Death or Time. He had said as much, when thinking only of the Friend, in 1-17. Then he found himself infected with it. This explains much. The lines

My glasse shall not perswade me I am ould,
So long as youth and thou are of one date, (22)

while they do not yet deal directly with this theme of narcissism, contain an assumption of its existence. 24, again, which is not a satisfactory poem, is obsessed with this problem without actually stating it.

It is likely that on at least one occasion Shakespeare did have some kind of physical relationship with the Friend. The sonnets addressed to him, particularly 33-36, are difficult to explain on any other hypothesis. The sense of guilt is too clearly stated to justify an assumption that it merely arose from desire for physical contact; it is not neurotic enough for this. The Sonnets are, in fact, not neurotic at all; had they been written by a man who was tormented by no more than guilty thoughts, they would have been. Even if the Friend had been primarily responsible, Shakespeare's concern for his reputation, and his willingness to take the blame, are easily explainable on the grounds that, first, the Friend probably had a far greater social reputation than Shakespeare to maintain, and secondly, that Shakespeare was the older man. If it is true that he had been entrusted with the task of 'stimulating the imagination' of a man younger than himself with a view to marriage (and the first ten sonnets of the sequence seem to bear this out), and had instead himself entered into an 'unnatural' relationship with him, then no one will suggest that it would have been neurotic of him to feel guilt and shame. It is not easy to explain 36 on any other hypothesis than the physical one. Shakespeare's guilt clearly arose from something that had actually happened: in 34 he blames the Friend for it (and perhaps he was justified in so doing, though we need not go as far as Butler); in 35 he offers his personal forgiveness; in 36 he acknowledges his own responsibility.

37-126 tell us little more about what actually happened between the two men. It emerges from 40-42 that the Friend 'took over' his mistress, and this is again alluded to in 133-136, in the sequence to the Mistress. It is possible that most of this was written at about the same time as 40-42.

The 'story' that is unfolded in the *Sonnets,* then, except for the features outlined above, is mainly a psychological one. They are more appropriately described as the record of a developing psychological situation than the history of two love-affairs.

As well as providing a glossary and an elucidation of the difficult passages, I have tried in my Commentary to trace this development. But why should the record of a situation that even Butler admitted was 'squalid', with 'a cancerous taint', be of importance to anyone?

The answer to this question is manifold. The intimate record of the intimate experience of a man so worldly-wise, so articulate and so truth-possessed as Shakespeare is bound to be important. This is obvious. What is perhaps not so obvious as it ought to be is what the *Sonnets* represent. There is a habit among critics of looking for and invariably finding a 'philosophy of life' in any poetic work which is generally regarded as 'great'. In the case of *Paradise Lost* such critics are plainly right: Milton was undeniably trying to put forward a fully planned philosophy. A prose-logic underlies the poetry.

But was Shakespeare? And, in particular, was he doing so in the *Sonnets*? If we look for such a philosophy in them, or even for a solution, in terms accessible to the merely logical mind, to the human problems with which they are concerned, we are in danger of reading something into them that is not there. There is only one sonnet, 146, in which anything like a feeling of triumph over circumstances is expressed; but this sonnet is not about sex, it is not even connected with any of the others; nor is its proud spirit ever speciously injected into them. There need be little doubt that it was occasioned by the stresses and strains of Shakespeare's experiences with the Friend and the Mistress; but it is significant that it is a wholly anti-materialist poem. The solution it offers to the problem of human suffering is not in human terms, which are specifically rejected – out of hand. No one, I think, would deny that the *Sonnets* as a whole convey an overwhelming atmosphere of having been written by a man who desperately wanted to exist well: to learn how to live and love truly. They do indeed represent the articulate poetic diary of a person who was seeking such a solution – but it was not sought as something that could be put down on paper, but rather as something that could be lived. We can never hope to understand the *Sonnets* if we do not understand this. They are seldom considered, but almost always immediate, and their directness is sometimes so shocking that at first reading it seems to be obscurity. The inborn lyrical note of idealistic innocence and wonder is increasingly cut across by a sharp involuntary irony; and yet it is never engulfed. Shakespeare obstinately goes on loving the Friend: the corrupt young man inevitably becomes for the reader a symbol, a figure of the beloved; but we are able to respond only because Shakespeare's love for him remained real. He never became, for the poet, a figure to be worked upon for poetic purposes; when he became free of him, he wrote no more of him. Shakespeare reached a state of mind in which he desired his welfare without expecting to get anything in return: It may seem a small thing in comparison with a full-blown 'philosophy of life' composed as a substitute for the political power that a man could not achieve; but how Shakespeare arrived at this state of mind is the subject-matter of the *Sonnets*.

13

The principles upon which this text is based are few and simple. The original spelling has been preserved; only the typography has been modernized. That is to say: the modern 's' has been substituted for the confusing long 's', so like an 'f'; and 'v' becomes 'u' and vice versa; and 'i', where necessary, becomes 'j'.

The old spelling has been kept because it is felt that the modern reader of Shakespeare does not wish to have any kind of barrier placed between himself and what the poet actually wrote: the original text will act as a continual reminder to the reader that these poems were written in late Elizabethan times, not in his own. The authentic background is lacking in modernized editions: editors gratuitously superimpose a modern, standardized orthography upon one which has few set rules. The effects of this practice have been insidious and far-reaching: a non-Shakespearean orthography (not so serious in itself, except for its tendency to evoke a false atmosphere) leads an editor to try to make the punctuation conform to modern rules, and this often leads to distortion and impoverishment of the sense. The spelling in this edition has been altered only where there is an obvious misprint; all the spellings preserved here would have been tolerated in Shakespeare's time.

The punctuation of this text, likewise, closely follows that of Q, whose punctuation looks and feels right in its proper context; it looks, feels and is wrong when applied to a modern standardized text. A distinction should perhaps be drawn, however, between a whole-hearted 'defence' of the Q punctuation, and an edition that follows it as closely as possible. Punctuation did not mean half so much to Shakespeare and his contemporaries as it does to us. And certainly it usually meant less to Shakespeare himself than it did to, say, Jonson or Donne. Rules of punctuation had been formulated in 1561 on the continent, and Chambers tells us that these were not unlike our own; but there is little or no evidence that they were followed in England, even by the printing-houses. English grammarians of the time scarcely discuss the topic. There is hardly any Elizabethan 'copy' extant, but what there is suggests that the writer, if he thought about it at all, left the punctuation of the published work to the printer, probably as a matter of course. The writer of verse must have had more authority, but the extent of this is open to conjecture. To try to defend the punctuation of Q on a systematic basis would be as artificial as to re-punctuate it on modern lines; it can only be explained. It is of no use even to say that the conflict between rhetoric and logic in punctuation had not yet been resolved: there was little or no awareness that such a conflict existed.

Despite this state of affairs, which is admittedly puzzling to the modern reader, a re-punctuated text possesses little more value than a translation of the original. First, in order to punctuate according to modern rules, an editor is often forced to make up his mind about the meaning of the original. This means that the sense of the poem is narrowed down; it is often robbed of a multiplicity of meaning which may be an inherent part of it. Secondly, the rhythm is interfered with. Thirdly, it is plain that violence will be done to the complex structure, and to the original intention, of poetic language, when rules not in existence at the time of its composition are belatedly applied to it. The distortion achieved by modernizing is usually subtle, but the effect is cumulative. A comparison of the Shakespearean original with its modern equivalent reveals that the two are as different from one another as chalk from cheese. The modern edition all too often represents a semi-critical impression, by an editor, of his personal response to the original text.

Most of the puzzling features of the punctuation of Shakespeare's text may be explained by the fact that its chief function is to point the rhythm and to indicate emphasis. The first serious attempt to explain this was made by Percy Simpson in his *Shakespearean Punctuation* (1911) and it is still the best. Simpson performed an invaluable service in pointing out that the stopping in Shakespearean texts had been governed to a large extent by considerations of rhythm; he was mostly concerned, of course, with the Folio, but some of his examples are from the *Sonnets,* and they demonstrate convincingly the correctness of the original text. When this all-important aspect of it is understood, Shakespeare's stopping is seen to be more sensitive to the usually complex meaning of the text than anyone else's attempts to correct or modernize it. Much of the criticism directed at Simpson's book is, in Chambers's words, 'ill-conceived', and in fact Chambers's own discussion of it, a sympathetic one, in *William Shakespeare*, is the best corrective to some of its excesses.

The text offered here has been emended only where the punctuation or spelling of Q is the undoubted result of a misprint.

Malone noted fifteen errors of 'their' for 'thy', in 26.12, 27.10, 35.8, 37.7, 43.11, 45.12, 46.3,8 and 13, 69.5, 70.6, 128.11 and 14. All these emendations, except 37.7, have been accepted in the present text. Malone thought that the confusion arose from the use of the abbreviations 'y^r' for 'their' and 'y^i' for 'thy'; Brooke, in his 1936 edition, explained it by suggesting that the copy had 'thie', and that if 'the final stroke of the "e" terminated in a small tremulous hook, the word would have resembled "their"...'

In short, then, this text sets out to do no more than to correct obvious misprints. There is little doubt that in a few places it might have been clarified; but it seems unsafe to attempt this in the absence of Shakespeare himself. All variations from Q have been noted at the foot of the sonnet in question. The entry in italics refers to the present text; that in roman gives the Q reading.

The variations to be found among the thirteen extant copies of Q are trifling. At 47, 10 the A. S. W. Rosenbach copy apparently has 'selfe' where the rest have 'seife'; 116 is wrongly numbered except in one of the two copies in the Bodleian Library. I have adopted these correct readings without a note. I have also changed 'whẽ' at 33, 14, to 'when' without a note. Five other obvious small errors are peculiar to certain copies; I have not listed these.

Catchwords and the large initial capitals and small capitals that usually characterize the first two letters respectively of each sonnet have been ignored.

TO.THE.ONLIE.BEGETTER.OF.
THESE.INSVING.SONNETS.
Mr.W.H. ALL.HAPPINESSE.
AND.THAT.ETERNITIE.
PROMISED.

BY.

OVR.EVER-LIVING.POET.

WISHETH.

THE.WELL-WISHING.
ADVENTVRER.IN.
SETTING.
FORTH.

T. T.

The Dedication, reproduced from the British Museum Bright Copy of Q.

1

From fairest creatures we desire increase,
That thereby beauties *Rose* might never die,
But as the riper should by time decease,
His tender heire might beare his memory:
But thou contracted to thine owne bright eyes,
Feed'st thy lights flame with selfe substantiall fewell,
Making a famine where aboundance lies,
Thy selfe thy foe, to thy sweet selfe too cruell:
Thou that art now the worlds fresh ornament,
And only herauld to the gaudy spring,
Within thine owne bud buriest thy content,
And tender chorle makst wast in niggarding
  Pitty the world, or else this glutton be,
  To eate the worlds due, by the grave and thee.

Q omits number of Sonnet.

2

When fortie Winters shall beseige thy brow,
And digge deep trenches in thy beauties field,
Thy youthes proud livery so gaz'd on now,
Wil be a totter'd weed of smal worth held:
Then being askt, where all thy beautie lies,
Where all the treasure of thy lusty daies;
To say within thine owne deepe sunken eyes,
Were an all-eating shame, and thriftlesse praise.
How much more praise deserv'd thy beauties use,
If thou couldst answere this faire child of mine
Shall sum my count, and make my old excuse
Prooving his beautie by succession thine.
  This were to be new made when thou art ould,
  And see thy blood warme when thou feel'st it could.

14 *could.* could,

3

Looke in thy glasse and tell the face thou vewest,
Now is the time that face should forme an other,
Whose fresh repaire if now thou not renewest,
Thou doo'st beguile the world, unblesse some mother.
For where is she so faire whose un-eard wombe
Disdaines the tillage of thy husbandry?
Or who is he so fond will be the tombe,
Of his selfe love to stop posterity?
Thou art thy mothers glasse and she in thee
Calls backe the lovely Aprill of her prime,
So thou through windowes of thine age shalt see
Dispight of wrinkles this thy goulden time.
  But if thou live remembred not to be,
  Die single and thine Image dies with thee.

4

Unthrifty lovelinesse why dost thou spend,
Upon thy selfe thy beauties legacy?
Natures bequest gives nothing but doth lend,
And being franck she lends to those are free:
Then beautious nigard why doost thou abuse,
The bountious largesse given thee to give?
Profitles userer why doost thou use
So great a summe of summes yet can'st not live?
For having traffike with thy selfe alone,
Thou of thy selfe thy sweet selfe dost deceave,
Then how when nature calls thee to be gone,
What acceptable *Audit* can'st thou leave?
  Thy unus'd beauty must be tomb'd with thee,
  Which used lives th'executor to be.

5

Those howers that with gentle worke did frame
The lovely gaze where every eye doth dwell
Will play the tirants to the very same,
And that unfaire which fairely doth excell:
For never resting time leads Summer on
To hidious winter and confounds him there,
Sap checkt with frost and lustie leav's quite gon.
Beauty ore-snow'd and barenes every where:
Then were not summers distillation left
A liquid prisoner pent in walls of glasse,
Beauties effect with beauty were bereft,
Nor it nor noe remembrance what it was.
  But flowers distil'd though they with winter meete,
  Leese but their show, their substance still lives sweet.

1 *frame* frame, 5 *on* on, 8 *every where:* every where,

6

Then let not winters wragged hand deface,
In thee thy summer ere thou be distil'd:
Make sweet some viall; treasure thou some place,
With beauties treasure ere it be selfe kil'd:
That use is not forbidden usery,
Which happies those that pay the willing lone;
That's for thy selfe to breed an other thee,
Or ten times happier be it ten for one,
Ten times thy selfe were happier then thou art,
If ten of thine ten times refigur'd thee,
Then what could death doe if thou should'st depart,
Leaving thee living in posterity?
  Be not selfe-wild for thou art much too faire,
  To be deaths conquest and make wormes thine heire.

4 *beauties* beautits

7

Loe in the Orient when the gracious light,
Lifts up his burning head, each under eye
Doth homage to his new appearing sight,
Serving with lookes his sacred majesty,
And having climb'd the steepe up heavenly hill,
Resembling strong youth in his middle age,
Yet mortall lookes adore his beauty still,
Attending on his goulden pilgrimage
But when from high-most pich with wery car,
Like feeble age he reeleth from the day,
The eyes (fore dutious) now converted are
From his low tract and looke an other way:
  So thou, thy selfe out-going in thy noon:
  Unlok'd on diest unlesse thou get a sonne.

8

Musick to heare, why hear'st thou musick sadly?
Sweets with sweets warre not, joy delights in joy:
Why lov'st thou that which thou receavst not gladly,
Or else receav'st with pleasure thine annoy?
If the true concord of well tuned sounds,
By unions married do offend thine eare,
They do but sweetly chide thee, who confounds
In singlenesse the parts that thou should'st beare
Marke how one string, sweet husband to an other,
Strikes each in each by mutuall ordering;
Resembling sier, and child, and happy mother,
Who all in one, one pleasing note do sing:
  Whose speechlesse song being many, seeming one,
  Sings this to thee: thou single wilt prove none.

1 *sadly?* sadly, 9 string, string, 14 *thee*: thee

9

Is it for feare to wet a widdowes eye,
That thou consum'st thy selfe in single life?
Ah; if thou issulesse shalt hap to die,
The world will waile thee like a makelesse wife,
The world wilbe thy widdow and still weepe,
That thou no forme of thee hast left behind;
When every privat widdow well may keepe,
By childrens eyes, her husbands shape in minde:
Looke what an unthrift in the world doth spend
Shifts but his place, for still the world injoyes it
But beauties waste hath in the world an end,
And kept unusde the user so destroyes it:
  No love toward others in that bosome sits
  That on himselfe such murdrous shame commits.

10

For shame deny that thou bear'st love to any
Who for thy selfe art so unprovident;
Graunt if thou wilt, thou art belov'd of many,
But that thou none lov'st is most evident:
For thou art so possest with murdrous hate,
That gainst thy selfe thou stickst not to conspire,
Seeking that beautious roofe to ruinate
Which to repaire should be thy chiefe desire:
O change thy thought, that I may change my minde,
Shall hate be fairer log'd then gentle love?
Be as thy presence is, gracious and kind,
Or to thy selfe at least kind harted prove,
  Make thee an other selfe for love of me,
  That beauty still may live in thine or thee.

2 *unprovident*; unprovident   11 *is*, is

11

As fast as thou shalt wane so fast thou grow'st,
In one of thine, from that which thou departest,
And that fresh bloud which yongly thou bestow'st,
Thou maist call thine, when thou from youth convertest,
Herein lives wisdome, beauty, and increase,
Without this, follie, age, and could decay,
If all were minded so, the times should cease,
And threescoore yeare would make the world away
Let those whom nature hath not made for store,
Harsh, featurelesse, and rude, barrenly perrish,
Looke whom she best indow'd, she gave thee more;
Which bountious guift thou shouldst in bounty cherrish,
  She carv'd thee for her scale, and ment therby,
  Thou shouldst print more, not let that coppy die.

6 *this*: this, 11 *thee:* the.

12

When I doe count the clock that tels the time,
And see the brave day sunck in hidious night,
When I behold the violet past prime,
And sable curls or silver'd ore with white:
When lofty trees I see barren of leaves,
Which erst from heat did canopie the herd
And Sommers greene all girded up in sheaves
Borne on the beare with white and bristly beard
Then of thy beauty do I question make
That thou among the wastes of time must goe,
Since sweets and beauties do them-selves forsake,
And die as fast as they see others grow,
  And nothing gainst Times sieth can make defence
  Save breed to brave him, when he takes thee hence.

13

O that you were your selfe, but love you are
No longer yours, then you your selfe here live,
Against this cumming end you should prepare,
And your sweet semblance to some other give.
So should that beauty which you hold in lease
Find no determination, then you were
Your selfe again after your selfes decease,
When your sweet issue your sweet forme should bears
Who lets so faire a house fall to decay,
Which husbandry in honour might uphold,
Against the stormy gusts of winters day
And barren rage of deaths eternall cold?
  O none but unthrifts, deare my love you know,
  You had a Father, let your Son say so.

7 *Your selfe* You selfe

14

Not from the stars do I my judgement plucke,
And yet me thinkes I have Astronomy,
But not to tell of good, or evil lucke,
Of plagues, of dearths, or seasons quallity,
Nor can I fortune to breefe mynuits tell;
Pointing to each his thunder, raine and winde,
Or say with Princes if it shal go wel
By oft predict that I in heaven finde.
But from thine eies my knowledge I derive,
And constant stars in them I read such art
As truth and beautie shal together thrive
If from thy selfe, to store thou wouldst convert:
  Or else of thee this I prognosticate,
  Thy end is Truthes and Beauties doome and date.

15

When I consider every thing that growes
Holds in perfection but a little moment.
That this huge stage presenteth nought but showes
Whereon the Stars in secret influence comment.
When I perceive that men as plants increase,
Cheared and checkt even by the selfe-same skie:
Vaunt in their youthfull sap, at height decrease,
And were their brave state out of memory.
Then the conceit of this inconstant stay,
Sets you most rich in youth before my sight,
Where wastfull time debateth with decay
To change your day of youth to sullied night,
  And all in war with Time for love of you
  As he takes from you, I ingraft you new.

16

But wherefore do not you a mightier waie
Make warre uppon this bloudie tirant time?
And fortifie your selfe in your decay
With meanes more blessed then my barren rime?
Now stand you on the top of happie houres,
And many maiden gardens yet unset,
With vertuous wish would beare your living flowers,
Much liker then your painted counterfeit:
So should the lines of life that life repaire
Which this (Times pensel or my pupill pen)
Neither in inward worth nor outward faire
Can make you live your selfe in eies of men.
  To give away your selfe, keeps your selfe still,
  And you must live drawne by your owne sweet skill.

12 *men.* men,   14 *skill.* skill,

17

Who will beleeve my verse in time to come
If it were fild with your most high deserts?
Though yet heaven knowes it is but as a tombe
Which hides your life, and shewes not halfe your parts
If I could write the beauty of your eyes,
And in fresh numbers number all your graces,
The age to come would say this Poet lies,
Such heavenly touches nere toucht earthly faces.
So should my papers (yellowed with their age)
Be scorn'd, like old men of lesse truth then tongue,
And your true rights be termd a Poets rage,
And stretched miter of an Antique song.
  But were some childe of yours alive that time,
  You should live twise in it, and in my rime.

18

Shall I compare thee to a Summers day?
Thou art more lovely and more temperate
Rough windes do shake the darling buds of Maie,
And Sommers lease hath all too short a date:
Sometime too hot the eye of heaven shines,
And often is his gold complexion dimm'd,
And every faire from faire some-time declines,
By chance, or natures changing course untrim'd:
But thy eternall Sommer shall not fade,
Nor loose possession of that faire thou ow'st,
Nor shall death brag thou wandr'st in his shade,
When in eternall lines to time thou grow'st,
  So long as men can breath or eyes can see,
  So long lives this, and this gives life to thee.

14 *thee.* thee,

19

Devouring time blunt thou the Lyons pawes,
And make the earth devoure her owne sweet brood,
Plucke the keene teeth from the fierce Tygers jawes,
And burne the long liv'd Phænix in her blood,
Make glad and sorry seasons as thou fleet'st,
And do what ere thou wilt swift-footed time
To the wide world and all her fading sweets:
But I forbid thee one most hainous crime,
O carve not with thy bowers my loves faire brow,
Nor draw noe lines there with thine antique pen,
Him in thy course untainted doe allow,
For beauties patterne to succeding men.
  Yet doe thy worst ould Time dispight thy wrong,
  My love shall in my verse ever live young.

3 *jawes* yawes

20

A womans face with natures owne hand painted,
Haste thou the Master Mistris of my passion,
A womans gentle hart but not acquainted
With shifting change as is false womens fashion,
An eye more bright then theirs, lesse false in rowling:
Gilding the object where-upon it gazeth,
A man in hew all *Hews* in his controwling,
Which steales mens eyes and womens soules amaseth.
And for a woman wert thou first created,
Till nature as she wrought thee fell a dotinge,
And by addition me of thee defeated,
By adding one thing to my purpose nothing.
  But since she prickt thee out for womens pleasure,
  Mine be thy love and thy loves use their treasure.

21

So is it not with me as with that Muse,
Stird by a painted beauty to his verse,
Who heaven it selfe for ornament doth use,
And every faire with his faire doth reherse,
Making a coopelment of proud compare
With Sunne and Moone, with earth and seas rich gems:
With Aprills first borne flowers and all things rare,
That heavens gyre in this huge rondure hems,
O let me true in love but truly write,
And then beleeve me, my love is as faire,
As any mothers childe, though not so bright
As those gould candells fixt in heavens ayer:
  Let them say more that like of heare-say well,
  I will not prayse that purpose not to sell.

22

My glasse shall not perswade me I am ould,
So long as youth and thou are of one date,
But when in thee times forrwes I behould,
Then look I death my daies should expiate.
For all that beauty that doth cover thee,
Is but the seemely rayment of my heart,
Which in thy brest doth live, as thine in me,
How can I then be elder then thou art?
O therefore love be of thy selfe so wary,
As I not for my selfe, but for thee will,
Bearing thy heart which I will keepe so chary
As tender nurse her babe from faring ill,
  Presume not on thy heart when mine is slaine,
  Thou gav'st me thine not to give backe againe.

23

As an unperfect actor on the stage,
Who with his feare is put besides his part,
Or some fierce thing repleat with too much rage,
Whose strengths abondance weakens his owne heart;
So I for feare of trust, forget to say,
The perfect ceremony of loves right,
And in mine owne loves strength seeme to decay,
Ore-charg'd with burthen of mine owne loves might:
O let my books be then the eloquence,
And domb presagers of my speaking brest,
Who pleade for love, and look for recompence,
More then that tonge that more hath more exprest.
O learne to read what silent love hath writ,
To heare with eies belongs to loves fine wit.

14 *with… wit*, wit… wiht

24

Mine eye hath play'd the painter and hath steeld,
Thy beauties forme in table of my heart,
My body is the frame wherein 'tis held,
And perspective it is best Painters art.
For through the Painter must you see his skill,
To finde where your true Image pictur'd lies,
Which in my bosomes shop is hanging stil,
That hath his windowes glazed with thine eyes:
Now see what good-turnes eyes for eies have done,
Mine eyes have drawne thy shape, and thine for me
Are windowes to my brest, where-through the Sun
Delights to peepe, to gaze therein on thee.
  Yet eyes this cunning want to grace their art
  They draw but what they see, know not the hart.

3 *'tis* ti's   12 *thee.* thee

25

Let those who are in favor with their stars,
Of publike honour and proud titles bost,
Whilst I whome fortune of such tryumph bars
Unlookt for joy in that I honour most;
Great Princes favorites their faire leaves spread,
But as the Marygold at the suns eye,
And in them-selves their pride lies buried,
For at a frowne they in their glory die.
The painefull warrier famosed for worth,
After a thousand victories once foild,
Is from the booke of honour rased quite,
And all the rest forgot for which he toild:
  Then happy I that love and am beloved
  Where I may not remove, nor be removed.

26

Lord of my love, to whome in vassalage
Thy merrit hath my dutie strongly knit;
To thee I send this written ambassage
To witnesse duty, not to skew my wit.
Duty so great, which wit so poore as mine
May make seeme bare, in wanting words to shew it;
But that I hope some good conceipt of thine
In thy soules thought (all naked) will bestow it:
Til whatsoever star that guides my moving,
Points on me graciously with faire aspect,
And puts apparrell on my tottered loving,
To show me worthy of thy sweet respect,
  Then may I dare to boast how I doe love thee,
  Till then, not show my head where thou maist prove me.

12 *thy* their   14 *me*. me

27

Weary with toyle, I hast me to my bed,
The deare repose for lims with travaill tired,
But then begins a journy in my head
To worke my mind, when boddies work's expired.
For then my thoughts (from far where I abide)
Intend a zelous pilgrimage to thee,
And keepe my drooping eye-lids open wide,
Looking on darknes which the blind doe see.
Save that my soules imaginary sight
Presents thy shaddoe to my sightles view,
Which like a jewell (hunge in gastly night)
Makes blacke night beautious, and her old face new.
  Loe thus by day my lims, by night my mind,
  For thee, and for my selfe, noe quiet finde.

10 *thy* their

28

How can I then returne in happy plight
That am debard the benifit of rest?
When daies oppression is not eazd by night,
But day by night and night by day oprest.
And each (though enimes to ethers raigne)
Doe in consent shake hands to torture me,
The one by toyle, the other to complaine
How far I toyle, still farther off from thee.
I tell the Day to please him thou art bright,
And do'st him grace when clouds doe blot the heaven:
So flatter I the swart complexiond night,
When sparkling stars twire not thou guil'st th' eaven.
  But day doth daily draw my sorrowes longer,
  And night doth nightly make greefes length seeme stronger.

14 *stronger.* stronger

29

When in disgrace with Fortune and mens eyes,
I all alone beweepe my out-cast state,
And trouble deafe heaven with my bootlesse cries,
And looke upon my selfe and curse my fate,
Wishing me like to one more rich in hope,
Featur'd like him, like him with friends possest,
Desiring this mans art, and that mans skope,
With what I most injoy contented least,
Yet in these thoughts my selfe almost despising,
Haplye I thinke on thee, and then my state,
(Like to the Larke at breake of day arising)
From sullen earth sings himns at Heavens gate,
  For thy sweet love remembred such welth brings,
  That then I skorne to change my state with Kings.

4 *fate*, fate.

30

When to the Sessions of sweet silent thought,
I sommon up remembrance of things past,
I sigh the lacke of many a thing I sought,
And with old woes new waile my deare times waste:
Then can I drowne an eye (un-us'd to flow)
For precious friends hid in deaths dateles night,
And weepe a fresh loves long since canceld woe,
And mone th'expence of many a vannisht sight.
Then can I greeve at greevances fore-gon,
And heavily from woe to woe tell ore
The sad account of fore-bemoned move,
Which I new pay as if not payd before.
  But if the while I thinke on thee (deare friend)
  All losses are restord, and sorrowes end.

31

Thy bosome is indeared with all hearts,
Which I by lacking have supposed dead,
And there raignes Love and all Loves loving parts,
And all those friends which I thought buried.
How many a holy and obsequious teare
Hath deare religious love stolne from mine eye,
As interest of the dead, which now appeare,
But things remov'd that hidden in there lie.
Thou art the grave where buried love doth live,
Hung with the tropheis of my lovers gon,
Who all their parts of me to thee did give,
That due of many, now is thine alone.
  Their images I lov'd, I view in thee,
  And thou (all they) hast all the all of me.

32

If thou survive my well contented daie,
When that churle death my bones with dust shall cover
And shalt by fortune once more re-survay:
These poore rude lines of thy deceased Lover:
Compare them with the bett'ring of the time,
And though they be out-stript by every pen,
Reserve them for my love, not for their rime,
Exceeded by the hight of happier men.
Oh then voutsafe me but this loving thought,
Had my friends Muse growne with this growing age,
A dearer birth then this his love had brought
To march in ranckes of better equipage:
  But since he died and Poets better prove,
  Theirs for their stile ile read, his for his love.

33

Full many a glorious morning have I seene,
Flatter the mountaine tops with soveraine eie,
Kissing with golden face the meddowes greener
Guilding pale streames with heavenly alcumy:
Anon permit the basest cloudes to ride,
With ougly rack on his celestiall face,
And from the for-lorne world his visage hide
Stealing unseene to west with this disgrace:
Even so my Sunne one early morne did shine,
With all triumphant splendor on my brow,
But out alack, he was but one houre mine,
The region cloude hath mask'd him from me now.
  Yet him for this, my love no whit disdaineth,
  Suns of the world may staine, when heavens sun staineth.

14 *staineth.* stainteh.

34

Why didst thou promise such a beautious day,
And make me travaile forth without my cloake,
To let bace cloudes ore-take me in my way,
Hiding thy brav'ry in their rotten smoke.
Tis not enough that through the cloude thou breake,
To dry the raine on my storme-beaten face,
For no man well of such a salve can speake,
That heales the wound, and cures not the disgrace:
Nor can thy shame give phisicke to my griefe,
Though thou repent, yet I have still the losse,
Th'offenders sorrow lends but weake reliefe
To him that beares the strong offenses losse.
  Ah but those teares are pearle which thy love sheeds,
  And they are ritch, and ransome all ill deeds.

35

No more bee greev'd at that which thou bast done,
Roses have thornes, and silver fountaines mud,
Cloudes and eclipses staine both Moone and Sunne,
And loathsome canker lives in sweetest bud.
All men make faults, and even I in this,
Authorizing thy trespas with compare,
My selfe corrupting salving thy amisse,
Excusing thy sins more then thy sins are:
For to thy sensuall fault I bring in sence,
Thy adverse party is thy Advocate,
And gainst my selfe a lawfull plea commence,
Such civill war is in my love and hate,
  That I an accessary needs must be,
  To that sweet theefe which sourely robs from me.

8 *thy... thy* their... their 14 *me.* me,

36

Let me confesse that we two must be twaine,
Although our undevided loves are one:
So shall those blots that do with me remaine,
Without thy helpe, by me be borne alone.
In our two loves there is but one respect,
Though in our lives a seperable spight,
Which though it alter not loves sole effect,
Yet doth it steale sweet houres from loves delight,
I may not ever-more acknowledge thee,
Least my bewailed guilt should do thee shame,
Nor thou with publike kindnesse honour me,
Unlesse thou take that honour from thy name:
  But doe not so, I love thee in such sort,
  As thou being mine, mine is thy good report.

37

As a decrepit father takes delight,
To see his active childe do deeds of youth,
So I, made lame by Fortunes dearest spight
Take all my comfort of thy worth and truth.
For whether beauty, birth, or wealth, or wit,
Or any of these all, or all, or more
Intitled in their parts, do crowned sit,
I make my love ingrafted to this store:
So then I am not lame, poore, nor dispis'd,
Whilst that this shadow doth such substance give,
That I in thy abundance am suffic'd,
And by a part of all thy glory live:
  Looke what is best, that best I wish in thee,
  This wish I have, then ten times happy me.

38

How can my Muse want subject to invent
While thou dost breath that poor'st into my verse,
Thine owne sweet argument, to excellent,
For every vulgar paper to rehearse:
Oh give thy selfe the thankes if ought in me,
Worthy perusal stand against thy sight,
For who's so dumbe that cannot write to thee,
When thou thy self: dost give invention light?
Be thou the tenth Muse, ten times more in worth
Then those old nine which rimers invocate,
And he that calls on thee, let him bring forth
Eternal numbers to out-live long date.
  If my slight Muse doe please these curious daies,
  The paine be mine, but thine shal be the praise.

39

Oh how thy worth with manners may I singe,
When thou art all the better part of me?
What can mine owne praise to mine owne selfe bring;
And what is't but mine owne when I praise thee,
Even for this, let us devided live,
And our deare love loose name of single one,
That by this seperation I may give:
That due to thee which thou deserv'st alone:
Oh absence what a torment wouldst thou prove,
Were it not thy soure leisure gave sweet leave,
To entertaine the time with thoughts of love,
Which time and thoughts so sweetly dost deceive.
And that thou teachest how to make one twaine,
By praising him here who doth hence remaine.

40

Take all my loves, my love, yea take them all,
What hast thou then more then thou hadst before?
No love, my love, that thou maist true love call,
All mine was thine, before thou hadst this more:
Then if for my love, thou my love receivest,
I cannot blame thee, for my love thou usest,
But yet be blam'd, if thou this selfe deceavest
By wilfull taste of what thy selfe refusest.
I doe forgive thy robb'rie gentle theefe
Although thou steale thee all my poverty:
And yet love knowes it is a greater griefe
To beare loves wrong, then hates knowne injury.
  Lascivious grace, in whom all il wel showes,
  Kill me with spights yet we must not be foes.

41

Those pretty wrongs that liberty commits,
When I am some-time absent from thy heart,
Thy beautie, and thy yeares full well befits,
For still temptation followes where thou art.
Gentle thou art, and therefore to be wonne,
Beautious thou art, therefore to be assailed.
And when a woman woes, what womans sonne,
Will sourely leave her till he have prevailed.
Aye me, but yet thou mighst my seate forbeare,
And chide thy beauty, and thy straying youth,
Who lead thee in their ryot even there
Where thou art forst to breake a two-fold truth
  Hers by thy beauty tempting her to thee,
  Thine by thy beautie beeing false to me.

42

That thou hast her it is not all my griefe,
And yet it may be said I lov'd her deerely,
That she hath thee is of my wayling cheefe,
A losse in love that touches me more neerely.
Loving offendors thus I will excuse yee,
Thou doost love her, because thou knowst I love her,
And for my sake even so doth she abuse me,
Suffring my friend for my sake to approove her,
If I loose thee, my losse is my loves gaine,
And loosing her, my friend hath found that losse,
Both finds each other, and I loose both twaine,
And both for my sake lay on me this crosse,
  But here's the joy, my friend and I are one,
  Sweete flattery, then she loves but me alone.

43

When most I winke then doe mine eyes best see,
For all the day they view things unrespected,
But when I sleepe, in dreames they looke on thee,
And darkely bright, are bright in darke directed.
Then thou whose shaddow shaddowes doth make bright,
How would thy shadowes forme, forme happy show,
To the cleere day with thy much cleerer light,
When to un-seeing eyes thy shade shines so?
How would (I say) mine eyes be blessed made,
By looking on thee in the living day?
When in dead night thy faire imperfect shade,
Through heavy sleepe on sightlesse eyes doth stay?
  All dayes are nights to see till I see thee,
  And nights bright daies when dreams do shew thee me.

11 *thy* their   14 *me*. me,

44

If the dull substance of my flesh were thought,
Injurious distance should not stop my way,
For then dispight of space I would be brought,
From limits farre remote, where thou doost stay,
No matter then although my foote did stand
Upon the farthest earth remoov'd from thee,
For nimble thought can jumpe both sea and land,
As soone as thinke the place where he would be.
But ah, thought kills me that I am not thought
To leape large lengths of miles when thou art gone,
But that so much of earth and water wrought,
I must attend, times leasure with my mone.
  Receiving naught by elements so sloe,
  But heavie teares, badges of eithers woe.

13 *naught* naughts

45

The other two, slight ayre, and purging fire,
Are both with thee, where ever I abide,
The first my thought, the other my desire,
These present absent with swift motion slide.
For when these quicker Elements are gone
In tender Embassie of love to thee,
My life being made of foure, with two alone,
Sinkes downe to death, opprest with melancholie.
Untill lives composition be recured,
By those swift messengers return'd from thee,
Who even but now come back againe assured,
Of thy faire health, recounting it to me.
  This told, I joy, but there no longer glad,
  I send them back againe and straight grow sad.

12 *thy* their

46

Mine eye and heart are at a mortall warre,
How to devide the conquest of thy sight,
Mine eye, my heart thy pictures sight would barre,
My heart, mine eye the freedome of that right,
My heart doth plead that thou in him doost lye,
(A closet never pearst with christall eyes)
But the defendant doth that plea deny,
And sayes in him thy faire appearance lyes.
To side this title is impannelled
A quest of thoughts, all tennants to the heart,
And by their verdict is determined
The cleere eyes moyitie, and the deare hearts part.
  As thus, mine eyes due is thy outward part,
  And my hearts right, thy inward love of heart.

3 *thy* their   4 *freedome* freeedome   8 *thy* their   13 *thy* their

47

Betwixt mine eye and heart a league is tooke,
And each doth good turnes now unto the other,
When that mine eye is famisht for a looke,
Or heart in love with sighes himselfe doth smother;
With my loves picture then my eye doth feast,
And to the painted banquet bids my heart:
An other time mine eye is my hearts guest,
And in his thoughts of love doth share a part.
So either by thy picture or my love,
Thy selfe away, are present still with me,
For thou nor farther then my thoughts canst move,
And I am still with them, and they with thee.
  Or if they sleepe, thy picture in my sight
  Awakes my heart, to hearts and eyes delight.

48

How carefull was I when I tooke my way,
Each trifle under truest barres to thrust,
That to my use it might un-used stay
From hands of falsehood, in sure wards of trust?
But thou, to whom my jewels trifles are,
Most worthy comfort, now my greatest griefe,
Thou best of deerest, and mine only care,
Art left the prey of every vulgar theefe.
Thee have I not lockt up in any chest,
Save where thou art not, though I feele thou art,
Within the gentle closure of my brest,
From whence at pleasure thou maist come and part,
  And even thence thou wilt be stolne I feare,
  For truth prooves theevish for a prize so deare.

49

Against that time (if ever that time come)
When I shall see thee frowne on my defects,
When as thy love hath cast his utmost summe,
Cauld to that audite by advis'd respects,
Against that time when thou shalt strangely passe,
And scarcely greete me with that sunne thine eye,
When love converted from the thing it was
Shall reasons finde of setled gravitie.
Against that time do I insconce me here
Within the knowledge of mine owne desart,
And this my hand, against my selfe upreare,
To guard the lawfull reasons on thy part,
  To leave poore me, thou hast the strength of lawes,
  Since why to love, I can alledge no cause.

50

How heavie doe I journey on the way,
When what I seeke (my wearie travels end)
Doth teach that ease and that repose to say
Thus farre the miles are measurde from thy friend.
The beast that beares me, tired with my woe,
Plods duly on, to beare that waight in me,
As if by some instinct the wretch did know
His rider lovd not speed being made from thee:
The bloody spurre cannot provoke him on,
That some-times anger thrusts into his hide,
Which heavily he answers with a grone,
More sharpe to me then spurring to his side,
  For that same grone doth put this in my mind,
  My greefe lies onward and my joy behind.

51

Thus can my love excuse the slow offence,
Of my dull bearer, when from thee I speed,
From where thou art, why shoulld I hast me thence,
Till I returne of posting is noe need.
O what excuse will my poore beast then find,
When swift extremity can seeme but slow,
Then should I spurre though mounted on the wind,
In winged speed no motion shall I know,
Then can no horse with my desire keepe pace,
Therefore desire (of perfects love being made)
Shall naigh noe dull flesh in his fiery race,
But love, for love, thus shall excuse my jade,
  Since from thee going, he went wilfull slow,
  Towards thee ile run, and give him leave to goe.

52

So am I as the rich whose blessed key,
Can bring him to his sweet up-locked treasure,
The which he will not ev'ry hower survay,
For blunting the fine point of seldome pleasure.
Therefore are feasts so sollemne and so rare,
Since sildom comming in the long yeare set,
Like stones of worth they thinly placed are,
Or captaine Jewells in the carconet.
So is the time that keepes you as my chest,
Or as the ward-robe which the robe doth hide,
To make some speciall instant speciall blest,
By new unfoulding his imprison'd pride.
Blessed are you whose worthinesse gives skope,
Being had to tryomph, being lackt to hope.

53

What is your substance, whereof are you made,
That millions of strange shaddowes on you tend?
Since every one, hath every one, one shade,
And you but one, can every shaddow lend:
Describe *Adonis* and the counterfet,
Is poorely immitated after you,
On *Hellens* cheeke all art of beautie set,
And you in *Grecian* tires are painted new:
Speake of the spring, and foyzon of the yeare,
The one doth shaddow of your beautie show,
The other as your bountie doth appeare,
And you in every blessed shape we know.
  In all externall grace you have some part,
  But you like none, none you for constant heart.

54

Oh how much more doth beautie beautious seeme,
By that sweet ornament which truth doth give,
The Rose lookes faire, but fairer we it deeme
For that sweet odor, which doth in it live:
The Canker bloomes have full as deepe a die,
As the perfumed tincture of the Roses,
Hang on such thornes, and play as wantonly,
When sommers breath their masked buds discloses:
But for their virtue only is their show,
They live unwoo'd, and unrespected fade,
Die to themselves. Sweet Roses doe not so,
Of their sweet deathes, are sweetest odours made:
  And so of you, beautious and lovely youth,
  When that shall vade, by verse distils your truth.

55

Not marble, nor the guilded monuments
Of Princes shall out-live this powrefull rime,
But you shall shine more bright in these contents
Then unswept stone, besmeer'd with sluttish time.
When wastefull warre shall *Statues* over-turne,
And broiles roote out the worke of masonry,
Nor *Mars* his sword, nor warres quick fire shall burne:
The living record of your memory.
Gainst death, and all oblivious enmity
Shall you pace forth, your praise shall stil finde roome,
Even in the eyes of all posterity
That weare this world out to the ending doome.
  So til the judgement that your selfe arise,
  You live in this, and dwell in lovers eies.

1 *monuments* monument, 9 *enmity* emnity

56

Sweet love renew thy force, be it not said
Thy edge should blunter be then apetite,
Which but too daie by feeding is alaied,
To morrow sharpned in his former might.
So love be thou, although too daie thou fill
Thy hungry eies, even till they winck with fulnesse,
Too morrow see againe, and doe not kill
The spirit of Love, with a perpetual dulnesse
Let this sad *Intrim* like the Ocean be
Which parts the shore, where two contracted new,
Come daily to the banckes, that when they see:
Returne of love, more blest may be the view.
  As cal it Winter, which being ful of care,
  Makes Somers welcome, thrice more wish'd, more rare.

57

Being your slave what should I doe but tend,
Upon the houres, and times of your desire?
I have no precious time at al to spend;
Nor services to doe til you require.
Nor dare I chide the world without end houre,
Whilst I (my soveraine) watch the clock for you,
Nor thinke the bitternesse of absence sowre,
When you have bid your servant once adieue.
Nor dare I question with my jealious thought,
Where you may be, or your affaires suppose,
But like a sad slave stay and thinke of nought
Save where you are, how happy you make those.
  So true a foole is love, that in your Will,
  (Though you doe any thing) he thinkes no ill.

58

That God forbid, that made me first your slave,
I should in thought controule your times of pleasure,
Or at your hand th'account of houres to crave,
Being your vassail bound to staie your leisure.
Oh let me suffer (being at your beck).
Th'imprison'd absence of your libertie,
And patience tame, to sufferance bide each check,
Without accusing you of injury.
Be where you list, your charter is so strong,
That you your selfe may priviledge your time
To what you will, to you it doth belong,
Your selfe to pardon of selfe-doing crime.
  I am to waite, though waiting so be hell,
  Not blame your pleasure be it ill or well.

59

If their bee nothing new, but that which is,
Hath beene before, how are our braines beguild,
Which laboring for invention beare amisse
The second burthen of a former child?
Oh that record could with a back-ward looke,
Even of five hundreth courses of the Sunne,
Show me your image in some antique booke,
Since minde at first in carrecter was done.
That I might see what the old world could say,
To this composed wonder of your frame,
Whether we are mended, or where better they,
Or whether revolution be the same.
  Oh sure I am the wits of former daies,
  To subjects worse have given admiring praise.

60

Like as the waves make towards the pibled shore,
So do our minuites hasten to their end,
Each changing place with that which goes before,
In sequent toile all forwards do contend.
Nativity once in the maine of light,
Crawles to maturity, wherewith being crown'd,
Crooked eclipses gainst his glory fight,
And time that gave, doth now his gift confound.
Time doth transfixe the florish set on youth,
And delves the paralels in beauties brow,
Feedes on the rarities of natures truth,
And nothing stands but for his sieth to mow.
  And yet to times in hope, my verse shall stand
  Praising thy worth, dispight his cruell hand.

5 *light*, light.

61

Is it thy wil, thy Image should keepe open
My heavy eielids to the weary night?
Dost thou desire my slumbers should be broken,
While shadowes like to thee do mocke my sight?
Is it thy spirit that thou send'st from thee
So farre from home into my deeds to prye,
To find out shames and idle houres in me,
The skope and tenure of thy Jelousie?
O no, thy love though much, is not so great,
It is my love that keepes mine eie awake,
Mine owne true love that doth my rest defeat,
To plaie the watch-man ever for thy sake.
  For thee watch I, whilst thou dost wake elsewhere,
  From me farre of, with others all to neere.

62

Sinne of self-love possesseth al mine eie,
And all my soule, and al my every part;
And for this sinne there is no remedie,
It is so grounded inward in my heart.
Me thinkes no face so gratious is as mine,
No shape so true, no truth of such account,
And for my selfe mine owne worth do define,
As I all other in all worths surmount.
But when my glasse shewes me my selfe indeed
Beated and chopt with tand antiquitie,
Mine owne selfe love quite contrary I read:
Selfe, so selfe loving were iniquity,
  T'is thee (my selfe) that for my selfe I praise,
  Painting my age with beauty of thy daies.

11 *read:* read   14 *daies*. daies

63

Against my love shall be as I am now
With times injurious hand chrusht and ore-worne,
When houres have dreind his blood and fild his brow
With lines and wrincles, when his youthfull morne
Hath travaild on to Ages steepie night,
And all those beauties whereof now he's King
Are vanishing, or vanisht out of sight,
Stealing away the treasure of his Spring.
For such a time do I now fortifie
Against confounding Ages cruell knife,
That he shall never cut from memory
My sweet loves beauty, though my lovers life.
  His beautie shall in these blacke lines be seene,
  And they shall live, and he in them still greene.

64

When I have seene by times fell hand defaced
The rich proud cost of outworne buried age,
When sometime loftie towers I see downe rased,
And brasse eternall slave to mortall rage.
When I have seene the hungry Ocean gaine
Advantage on the Kingdome of the shoare,
And the firme soile win of the watry maine,
Increasing store with losse, and losse with store.
When I have seene such interchange of state,
Or state it selfe confounded, to decay,
Ruine hath taught me thus to ruminate
That Time will come and take my love away.
  This thought is as a death which cannot choose
  But weepe to have, that which it feares to loose.

65

Since brasse, nor stone, nor earth, nor boundlesse sea,
But sad mortallity ore-swaies their power,
How with this rage shall beautie hold a plea,
Whose action is no stronger then a flower?
O how shall summers hunny breath hold out,
Against the wrackfull siedge of battring dayes,
When rocks impregnable are not so stoute,
Nor gates of steele so strong but time decayes?
O fearefull meditation, where alack,
Shall times best Jewell from times chest lie hid?
Or what strong hand can hold his swift foote back,
Or who his spoile of beautie can forbid?
  O none, unlesse this miracle have might,
  That in black inck my love may still shine bright.

12 *of* or

66

Tyr'd with all these for restfull death I cry,
As to behold desert a begger borne,
And needie Nothing trimd in jollitie,
And purest faith unhappily forsworne,
And gilded honor shamefully misplast,
And maiden vertue rudely strumpeted,
And right perfection wrongfully disgrac'd,
And strength by limping sway disabled,
And arte made tong-tide by authoritie,
And Folly (Doctor-like) controuling skill,
And simple-Truth miscalde Simplicitie,
And captive-good attending Captaine ill.
  Tyr'd with all these, from these would I be gone
  Save that to dye, I leave my love alone.

67

Ah wherefore with infection should he live,
And with his presence grace impietie,
That sinne by him advantage should atchive,
And lace it selfe with his societie?
Why should false painting immitate his cheeke,
And steale dead seeing of his living hew?
Why should poore beautie indirectly seeke,
Roses of shaddow, since his Rose is true?
Why should he live, now nature banckrout is,
Beggerd of blood to blush through lively vaines,
For she hath no exchecker now but his,
And proud of many, lives upon his gaines?
  O him she stores, to show what welth she had,
  In daies long since, before these last so bad.

68

Thus is his cheeke the map of daies out-worne,
When beauty liv'd and dy'ed as flowers do now,
Before these bastard signes of faire were borne,
Or durst inhabit on a living brow:
Before the goulden tresses of the dead,
The right of sepulchers, were shorne away,
To live a second life on second head,
Ere beauties dead fleece made another gay:
In him those holy antique howers are scene,
Without all ornament, it selfe and true,
Making no summer of an others greene,
Robbing no ould to dresse his beauty new,
  And him as for a map doth Nature store,
  To shew faulse Art what beauty was of yore.

69

Those parts of thee that the worlds eye doth view,
Want nothing that the thought of hearts can mend:
All toungs (the voice of soules) give thee that due,
Uttring bare truth, even so as foes Commend.
Thy outward thus with outward praise is crownd,
But those same toungs that give thee so thine owne,
In other accents doe this praise confound
By seeing farther then the eye hath showne.
They looke into the beauty of thy mind,
And that in guesse they measure by thy deeds,
Then churls their thoughts (although their eies were kind)
To thy faire flower ad the rancke smell of weeds,
  But why thy odor matcheth not thy show,
  The soyle is this, that thou doest common grow.

3 *due* end   5 *Thy* Their   4 *soyle* solye

70

That thou are blam'd shall not be thy defect,
For slanders marke was ever yet the faire,
The ornament of beauty is suspect,
A Crow that flies in heavens sweetest ayre.
So thou be good, slander doth but approve,
Thy worth the greater beeing woo'd of time,
For Canker vice the sweetest buds doth love,
And thou present'st a pure unstayined prime.
Thou hast past by the ambush of young daies,
Either not assayld, or victor beeing charg'd,
Yet this thy praise cannot be soe thy praise,
To tye up envy, evermore inlarged,
  If some suspect of ill maskt not thy show,
  Then thou alone kingdomes of hearts shouldst owe.

6 *Thy* Their

71

Noe Longer mourne for me when I am dead,
Then you shall heare the surly sullen bell
Give warning to the world that I am fled
From this vile world with vildest wormes to dwell:
Nay if you read this line, remember not,
The hand that writ it, for I love you so,
That I in your sweet thoughts would be forgot,
If thinking on me then should make you woe.
O if (I say) you looke upon this verse,
When I (perhaps) compounded am with clay,
Do not so much as my poore name reherse;
But let your love even with my life decay.
  Least the wise world should looke into your mone,
  And mocke you with me after I am gon.

72

O least the world should taske you to recite,
What merit liv'd in me that you should love
After my death (deare love) for get me quite,
For you in me can nothing worthy prove.
Unlesse you would devise some vertuous lye,
To doe more for me then mine owne desert,
And hang more praise upon deceased I,
Then nigard truth would willingly impart:
O least your true love may seeme falce in this,
That you for love speake well of me untrue,
My name be buried where my body is,
And live no more to shame nor me, nor you.
  For I am shamd by that which I bring forth,
  And so should you, to love things nothing worth.

73

That time of yeeare thou maist in me behold,
When yellow leaves, or none, or few doe hange
Upon those boughes which shake against the could,
Bare ruin'd quiers, where late the sweet birds sang.
In me thou seest the twi-light of such day,
As after Sun-set fadeth in the West,
Which by and by blacke night doth take away,
Deaths second selfe that seals up all in rest.
In me thou seest the glowing of such fire,
That on the ashes of his youth doth lye,
As the death bed, whereon it must expire,
Consum'd with that which it was nurrisht by.
  This thou percev'st, which makes thy love more strong,
  To love that well, which thou must leave ere long.

74

But be contented when that fell arest,
With out all bayle shall carry me away,
My life hath in this line some interest,
Which for memoriall still with thee shall stay.
When thou revewest this, thou doest revew,
The very part was consecrate to thee,
The earth can have but earth, which is his due,
My spirit is thine the better part of me,
So then thou hast but lost the dregs of life,
The pray of wormes, my body being dead,
The coward conquest of a wretches knife,
To base of thee to be remembered,
  The worth of that, is that which it containes,
  And that is this, and this with thee remaines.

75

So are you to my thoughts as food to life,
Of as sweet season'd shewers are to the ground;
And for the peace of you I hold such strife,
As twixt a miser and his wealth is found.
Now proud as an injoyer, and anon
Doubting the filching age will steale his treasure,
Now counting best to be with you alone,
Then betterd that the world may see my pleasure,
Some-time all ful with feasting on your sight,
And by and by cleane starved for a looke,
Possessing or pursuing no delight
Save what is had, or must from you be tooke.
  Thus do I pine and surfet day by day,
  Or gluttoning on all, or all away.

14 *away.* away

76

Why is my verse so barren of new pride?
So far from variation or quicke change?
Why with the time do I not glance aside
To new found methods, and to compounds strange?
Why write I still all one, ever the same,
And keepe invention in a noted weed,
That every word doth almost tell my name,
Shewing their birth, and where they did proceed?
O know sweet love I alwaies write of you,
And you and love are still my argument:
So all my best is dressing old words new,
Spending againe what is already spent:
  For as the Sun is daily new and old,
  So is my love still telling what is told.

7 *tell* fel 14 *told.* told,

77

Thy glasse will shew thee how thy beauties were,
Thy dyall how thy pretious mynuits waste,
The vacant leaves thy mindes imprint will beare,
And of this booke, this learning maist thou taste.
The wrinckles which thy glasse will truly show,
Of mouthed graves will give thee memorie,
Thou by thy dyals shady stealth maist know,
Times theevish progresse to eternitie.
Looke what thy memorie cannot containe,
Commit to these waste blacks, and thou shalt finde
Those children nurst, deliverd from thy braine,
To take a new acquaintance of thy minde.
  These offices, so oft as thou wilt looke,
  Shall profit thee, and much inrich thy booke.

78

So oft have I invok'd thee for my Muse.
And found such faire assistance in my verse,
As every *Alien* pen hath got my use,
And under thee their poesie disperse.
Thine eyes, that taught the dumbe on high to sing,
And heavie ignorance aloft to flie,
Have added fethers to the learneds wing,
And given grace a double Majestie.
Yet be most proud of that which I compile,
Whose influence is thine, and borne of thee,
In others workes thou doost but mend the stile,
And Arts with thy sweete graces graced be.
  But thou art all my art, and doost advance
  As high as learning, my rude ignorance.

79

Whilst I alone did call upon thy ayde,
My verse alone had all thy gentle grace,
But now my gracious numbers are decayde,
And my sick Muse doth give an other place.
I grant (sweet love) thy lovely argument
Deserves the travaile of a worthier pen,
Yet what of thee thy Poet doth invent,
He robs thee of, and payes it thee againe,
He lends thee vertue, and he stole that word,
From thy behaviour, beautie doth he give
And found it in thy cheeke: he can affoord
No praise to thee, but what in thee doth live.
  Then thanke him not for that which he doth say,
  Since what he owes thee, thou thy selfe doost pay.

14 *pay.* pay,

80

O how I faint when I of you do write,
Knowing a better spirit doth use your name,
And in the praise thereof spends all his might,
To make me toung-tide speaking of your fame.
But since your worth (wide as the Ocean is)
The humble as the proudest saile doth beare,
My sawsie barke (inferior farre to his)
On your broad maine doth wilfully appeare.
Your shallowest helpe will hold me up a floate,
Whilst he upon your soundlesse deepe doth ride,
Or (being wrackt) I am a worthlesse bote,
He of tall building, and of goodly pride.
  Then If he thrive and I be cast away,
  The worst was this, my love was my decay.

81

Or I shall live your Epitaph to make,
Or you survive when I in earth am rotten,
From hence your memory death cannot take,
Although in me each part will be forgotten.
Your name from hence immortall life shall have,
Though I (once gone) to all the world must dye,
The earth can yeeld me but a common grave,
When you intombed in mens eyes shall lye,
Your monument shall be my gentle verse,
Which eyes not yet created shall ore-read,
And toungs to be, your beeing shall rehearse,
When all the breathers of this world are dead,
  You still shall live (such vertue hath my Pen)
  Where breath most breaths, even in the mouths of men.

82

I grant thou wert not married to my Muse,
And therefore maiest without attaint ore-looke
The dedicated words which writers use
Of their faire subject, blessing every booke.
Thou art as faire in knowledge as in hew,
Finding thy worth a limmit past my praise,
And therefore art inforc'd to seeke anew,
Some fresher stampe of the time bettering dayes.
And do so love, yet when they have devisde,
What strained touches Rhethorick can lend,
Thou truly faire, wert truly simpathizde,
In true plaine words, by thy true telling friend.
  And their grosse painting might be better us'd,
  Where cheekes need blood, in thee it is abus'd.

83

I never saw that you did painting need,
And therefore to your faire no painting set,
I found (or thought I found) you did exceed,
The barren tender of a Poets debt:
And therefore have I slept in your report,
That you your selfe being extant well might show,
How farre a moderne quill doth come to short,
Speaking of worth, what worth in you doth grow,
This silence for my sinne you did impute,
Which shall be most my glory being dombe,
For I impaire not beautie being mute,
When others would give life, and bring a tombe.
  There lives more life in one of your faire eyes,
  Then both your Poets can in praise devise.

84

Who is it that sayes most, which can say more,
Then this rich praise, that you alone, are you,
In whose confine immured is the store,
Which should example where your equall grew,
Leane penurie within that Pen doth dwell,
That to his subject lends not some small glory,
But he that writes of you, if he can tell,
That you are you, so dignifies his story.
Let him but coppy what in you is writ,
Not making worse what nature made so cleere,
And such a counter-part shall fame his wit,
Making his stile admired every where.
  You to your beautious blessings adde a curse,
  Being fond on praise, which makes your praises worse.

85

My toung-tide Muse in manners holds her still,
While comments of your praise richly compil'd,
Reserve their Character with goulden quill,
And precious phrase by all the Muses fil'd.
I thinke good thoughts, whilst other write good wordes,
And like unlettered clarke still crie Amen,
To every Himne that able spirit affords,
In polisht forme of well refined pen.
Hearing you praisd, I say 'tis so, 'tis true,
And to the most of praise adde some-thing more,
But that is in my thought, whose love to you
(Though words come hind-most) holds his ranke before,
  Then others, for the breath of words respect,
  Me for my dombe thoughts, speaking in effect.

86

Was it the proud full saile of his great verse,
Bound for the prize of (all to precious) you,
That did my ripe thoughts in my braine inhearce,
Making their tombe the wombe wherein they grew?
Was it his spirit, by spirits taught to write,
Above a mortall pitch, that struck me dead?
No, neither he, nor his compiers by night
Giving him ayde, my verse astonished.
He nor that affable familiar ghost
Which nightly gulls him with intelligence,
As victors of my silence cannot boast,
I was not sick of any feare from thence.
  But when your countinance fild up his line,
  Then lackt I matter, that infeebled mine.

87

Farewell thou art too deare for my possessing,
And like enough thou knowst thy estimate,
The Charter of thy worth gives thee releasing:
My bonds in thee are all determinate.
For how do I hold thee but by thy granting,
And for that ritches where is my deserving?
The cause of this faire guift in me is wanting,
And so my pattent back againe is swerving.
Thy selfe thou gav'st, thy owne worth then not knowing,
Or mee to whom thou gav'st it, else mistaking,
So thy great guift upon misprision growing,
Comes home againe, on better judgement making.
  Thus have I had thee as a dreame doth flatter,
  In sleepe a King, but waking no such matter.

88

When thou shalt be dispos'd to set me light,
And place my merrit in the eie of skorne,
Upon thy side, against my selfe ile fight,
And prove thee virtuous, though thou art forsworne:
With mine owne weakenesse being best acquainted,
Upon thy part I can set downe a story
Of faults conceald, wherein I am attainted:
That thou in loosing me, shall win much glory:
And I by this wil be a gainer too,
For bending all my loving thoughts on thee,
The injuries that to myselfe I doe,
Doing thee vantage, duble vantage me.
  Such is my love, to thee I so belong,
  That for thy right, my selfe will beare all wrong.

1 *dispos'd* dispode

89

Say that thou didst forsake mee for some falt,
And I will comment upon that offence,
Speake of my lamenesse, and I straight will halt:
Against thy reasons making no defence.
Thou canst not (love) disgrace me halfe so ill,
To set a forme upon desired change,
As ile my selfe disgrace, knowing thy wil,
I will acquaintance strangle and looke strange:
Be absent from thy walkes and in my tongue,
Thy sweet beloved name no more shall dwell,
Least I (too much prophane) should do it wronge:
And haplie of our old acquaintance tell.
  For thee, against my selfe ile vow debate,
  For I must nere love him whom thou dost hate.

90

Then hate me when thou wilt, if ever, now,
Now while the world is bent my deeds to crosse,
Joyne with the spight of fortune, make me bow,
And doe not drop in for an after losse:
Ah doe not, when my heart hath scapte this sorrow,
Come in the rereward of a conquerd woe,
Give not a windy night a rainie morrow,
To linger out a purposd over-throw.
If thou wilt leave me, do not leave me last,
When other pettie griefes have done their spight,
But in the onset come, so shall I taste
At first the very worst of fortunes might.
  And other straines of woe, which now seeme woe,
  Compar'd with losse of thee, will not seeme so.

11 *shall* stall

91

Some glory in their birth, some in their skill,
Some in their wealth, some in their bodies force,
Some in their garments though new-fangled ill:
Some in their Hawkes and Hounds, some in their Horse
And every humor hath his adjunct pleasure,
Wherein it findes a joy above the rest,
But these perticulers are not my measure,
All these I better in one generall best.
Thy love is better then high birth to me,
Richer then wealth, prouder then garments cost,
Of more delight then Hawkes or Horses bee:
And having thee, of all mens pride I boast.
  Wretched in this alone, that thou maist take,
  All this away, and me most wretched make.

7 *better* bitter

92

But doe thy worst to steale thy selfe away,
For tearme of life thou art assured mine,
And life no longer then thy love will stay,
For it depends upon that love of thine.
Then need I not to feare the worst of wrongs,
When in the least of them my life hath end,
I see, a better state to me belongs
Then that, which on thy humor doth depend.
Thou canst not vex me with inconstant minde,
Since that my life on thy revolt doth lie,
Oh what a happy title do I finde,
Happy to have thy love, happy to die!
  But whats so blessed faire that feares no blot,
  Thou maist be falce, and yet I know it not.

93

So shall I live, supposing thou art true,
Like a deceived husband, so loves face,
May still seeme love to me, though alter'd new:
Thy lookes with me, thy heart in other place.
For their can live no hatred in thine eye,
Therefore in that I cannot know thy change,
In manies lookes, the falce hearts history
Is writ in moods and frounes and wrinckles strange.
But heaven in thy creation did decree,
That in thy face sweet love should ever dwell,
What ere thy thoughts, or thy hearts workings be,
Thy lookes should nothing thence, but sweetnesse tell.
  How like *Eaves* apple doth thy beauty grow,
  If thy sweet vertue answere not thy show.

94

They that have powre to hurt, and will doe none,
That doe not do the thing, they most do showe,
Who moving others, are themselves as stone,
Unmooved, could, and to temptation slow:
They rightly do inherrit heavens graces,
And husband natures ritches from expence,
They are the Lords and owners of their faces,
Others, but stewards of their excellence:
The sommers flowre is to the sommer sweet,
Though to it selfe, it onely live and die,
But if that flowre with base infection meete,
The basest weed out-braves his dignity:
  For sweetest things turne sowrest by their deedes,
  Lillies that fester, smell far worse then weeds.

95

How sweet and lovely dost thou make the shame,
Which like a canker in the fragrant Rose,
Doth spot the beautie of thy budding name?
Oh in what sweets doest thou thy sinnes inclose!
That tongue that tells the story of thy daies,
(Making lascivious comments on thy sport)
Cannot dispraise, but in a kinde of praise,
Naming thy name, blesses an ill report.
Oh what a mansion have those vices got,
Which for their habitation chose out thee,
Where beauties vaile doth cover every blot,
And all things turnes to faire, that eies can see!
  Take heed (deare heart) of this large priviledge,
  The hardest knife ill us'd doth loose his edge.

96

Some say thy fault is youth, some wantonesse,
Some say thy grace is youth and gentle sport,
Both grace and faults are lov'd of more and lesse:
Thou makst faults graces, that to thee resort:
As on the finger of a throned Queene,
The basest Jewell wil be well esteem'd:
So are those errors that in thee are seene,
To truths translated, and for true things deem'd.
How many Lambs might the sterne Wolfe betray,
If like a Lambe he could his lookes translate.
How many gazers mightst thou lead away,
If thou wouldst use the strength of all thy state?
  But doe not so, I love thee in such sort,
  As thou being mine, mine is thy good report.

97

How like a Winter hath my absence beene
From thee, the pleasure of the fleeting yeare?
What freezings have I felt, what darke daies seene?
What old Decembers barenesse every where?
And yet this time remov'd was sommers time,
And teeming Autumne big with ritch increase,
Bearing the wanton burthen of the prime,
Like widdowed wombes after their Lords decease:
Yet this aboundant issue seem'd to me,
But hope of Orphans, and un-fathered fruite,
For Sommer and his pleasures waite on thee,
And thou away, the very birds are mute.
  Or if they sing, tis with so dull a cheere,
  That leaves looke pale, dreading the Winters neere.

98

From you have I beene absent in the spring,
When proud pide Aprill (drest in all his trim)
Hath put a spirit of youth in every thing:
That heavie Saturne laught and leapt with him.
Yet nor the laies of birds, nor the sweet smell
Of different flowers in odor and in hew,
Could make me any summers story tell:
Or from their proud lap pluck them where they grew
Nor did I wonder at the Lillies white,
Nor praise the deepe vermillion in the Rose,
They weare but sweet, but figures of delight:
Drawne after you, you patterne of all those.
  Yet seem'd it Winter still, and you away,
  As with your shaddow I with these did play.

99

The forward violet thus did I chide,
Sweet theefe whence didst thou steale thy sweet that smels
If not from my loves breath, the purple pride,
Which on thy soft cheeke for complexion dwells?
In my loves veines thou hast too grosely died,
The Lillie I condemned for thy hand,
And buds of marjerom had stolne thy haire,
The Roses fearefully on thornes did stand,
One blushing shame, an other white dispaire:
A third nor red, nor white, had stolne of both,
And to his robbry had annext thy breath,
But for his theft in pride of all his growth
A vengful canker eate him up to death.
  More flowers I noted, yet I none could see,
  But sweet, or culler it had stolne from thee.

9 *One* Our

100

Where art thou Muse that thou forgetst so long,
To speake of that which gives thee all thy might?
Spendst thou thy furie on some worthlesse songe,
Darkning thy powre to lend base subjects light.
Returne forgetfull Muse, and straight redeeme,
In gentle numbers time so idely spent,
Sing to the eare that doth thy laies esteeme,
And gives thy pen both skill and argument.
Rise resty Muse, my loves sweet face survay,
If time have any wrincle graven there,
If any, be a *Satire* to decay,
And make times spoiles dispised every where.
  Give my love fame faster then time wasts life,
  So thou prevenst his sieth, and crooked knife.

101

Oh truant Muse what shalbe thy amends,
For thy neglect of truth in beauty di'd?
Both truth and beauty on my love depends:
So dost thou too, and therein dignifi'd:
Make answere Muse, wilt thou not haply saie,
Truth needs no collour with his collour fixt,
Beautie no pensell, beauties truth to lay:
But best is best, if never intermixt.
Because he needs no praise, wilt thou be dumb?
Excuse not silence so, for't lies in thee,
To make him much out-live a gilded tombe:
And to be praisd of ages yet to be.
  Then do thy office Muse, I teach thee how,
  To make him seeme long hence, as he showes now.

102

My love is strengthned though more weake in seeming
I love not lesse, thogh lesse the show appeare,
That love is marchandiz'd, whose ritch esteeming,
The owners tongue doth publish every where.
Our love was new, and then but in the spring,
When I was wont to greet it with my laies,
As *Philomell* in summers front doth singe,
And stops his pipe in growth of riper daies:
Not that the summer is lesse pleasant now
Then when her mournefull himns did hush the night,
But that wild musick burthens every bow,
And sweets growne common loose their deare delight.
  Therefore like her, I some-time hold my tongue:
  Because I would not dull you with my songe.

103

Alack what poverty my Muse brings forth,
That having such a skope to show her pride,
The argument all bare is of more worth
Then when it hath my added praise beside.
Oh blame me not if I no more can write!
Looke in your glasse and there appeares a face,
That over-goes my blunt invention quite,
Dulling my lines, and doing me disgrace.
Were it not sinfull then striving to mend,
To marre the subject that before was well,
For to no other passe my verses tend,
Then of your graces and your gifts to tell.
  And more, much more then in my verse can sit,
  Your owne glasse showes you, when you looke in it.

104

To me faire friend you never can be old,
For as you were when first your eye I eyde,
Such seemes your beautie still: Three Winters colde,
Have from the forrests shooke three summers pride,
Three beautious springs to yellow *Autumne* turned,
In processe of the seasons have I seene,
Three Aprill perfumes in three hot Junes burn'd,
Since first I saw you fresh which yet are greene.
Ah yet doth beauty like a Dyall hand,
Steale from his figure, and no pace perceiv'd,
So your sweete hew, which me thinkes still doth stand
Hath motion, and mine eye may be deceaved.
  For feare of which, heare this thou age unbred,
  Ere you were borne was beauties summer dead.

105

Let not my love be cal'd Idolatrie,
Nor my beloved as an Idoll show,
Since all alike my songs and praises be
To one, of one, still such, and ever so.
Kinde is my love to day, to morrow kinde,
Still constant in a wondrous excellence,
Therefore my verse to constancie confin'de,
One thing expressing, leaves out difference.
Faire, kinde, and true, is all my argument,
Faire, kinde and true, varrying to other words,
And in this change is my invention spent.
Three theams in one, which wondrous scope affords.
  Faire, kinde, and true, have often liv'd alone,
  Which three till now, never kept seate in one.

106

When in the Chronicle of wasted time,
I see discriptions of the fairest wights,
And beautie making beautifull old rime,
In praise of Ladies dead, and lovely Knights,
Then in the blazon of sweet beauties best,
Of hand, of foote, of lip, of eye, of brow,
I see their antique Pen would have exprest,
Even such a beauty as you maister now.
So all their praises are but prophesies
Of this our time, all you prefiguring,
And for they look'd but with devining eyes,
They had not still enough your worth to sing:
  For we which now behold these present dayes,
  Have eyes to wonder, but lack toungs to praise.

107

Not mine owne feares, nor the prophetick soule,
Of the wide world, dreaming on things to come,
Can yet the lease of my true love controule,
Supposde as forfeit to a confin'd doome.
The mortall Moone hath her eclipse indur'de,
And the sad Augurs mock their owne presage,
Incertenties now crowne them-selves assur'de,
And peace proclaimes Olives of endlesse age.
Now with the drops of this most balmie time,
My love lookes fresh, and death to me subscribes,
Since spight of him Ile live in this poore rime,
While he insults ore dull and speachlesse tribes.
  And thou in this shalt finde thy monument,
  When tyrants crests and tombs of brasse are spent.

108

What's in the braine that Inck may character,
Which hath not figur'd to thee my true spirit,
What's new to speake, what now to register,
That may expresse my love, or thy deare merit?
Nothing sweet boy, but yet like prayers divine,
I must each day say ore the very same,
Counting no old thing old, thou mine, I thine,
Even as when first I hallowed thy faire name.
So that eternall love in loves fresh case,
Waighes not the dust and injury of age,
Nor gives to necessary wrinckles place,
But makes antiquitie for aye his page,
  Finding the first conceit of love there bred,
  Where time and outward forme would shew it dead.

14 *dead.* dead,

109

O never say that I was false of heart,
Though absence seem'd my flame to quallifie,
As easie might I from my selfe depart,
As from my soule which in thy brest doth lye:
That is my home of love, if I have rang'd,
Like him that travels I returne againe,
Just to the time, not with the time exchang'd,
So that my selfe bring water for my staine,
Never beleeve though in my nature raign'd,
All frailties that besiege all kindes of blood,
That it could so preposterouslie be stain'd,
To leave for nothing all thy summe of good:
  For nothing this wide Universe I call,
  Save thou my Rose, in it thou art my all.

110

Alas 'tis true, I have gone here and there,
And made my selfe a motley to the view,
Gor'd mine own thoughts, sold cheap what is most deare,
Made old offences of affections new.
Most true it is, that I have lookt on truth
Asconce and strangely: But by all above,
These blenches gave my heart an other youth,
And worse essaies prov'd thee my best of love,
Now all is done, have what shall have no end,
Mine appetite I never more will grin'de
On newer proofe, to trie an older friend,
A God in love, to whom I am confin'd.
  Then give me welcome, next my heaven the best
  Even to thy pure and most most loving brest.

111

O for my sake doe you wish fortune chide,
The guiltie goddesse of my harmfull deeds,
That did not better for my life provide,
Then publick meanes which publick manners breeds.
Thence comes it that my name receives a brand,
And almost thence my nature is subdu'd
To what it workes in, like the Dyers hand,
Pitty me then, and wish I were renu'de,
Whilst like a willing pacient I will drinke,
Potions of Eysell gainst my strong infection,
No bitternesse that I will bitter thinke,
Nor double pennance to correct correction.
  Pittie me then deare friend, and I assure yee,
  Even that your pittie is enough to cure mee.

112

Your love and pittie doth th'impression fill,
Which vulgar scandall stampt upon my brow,
For what care I who calles me well or ill,
So you ore-greene my bad, my good alow?
You are my All the world and I must strive,
To know my shames and praises from your tounge,
None else to me, nor I to none alive,
That my steel'd sence or changes right or wrong,
In so profound *Abisme* I throw all care
Of others voyces, that my Adders sence,
To cryttick and to flatterer stopped are:
Marke how with my neglect I doe dispence
  You are so strongly in my purpose bred,
  That all the world besides me thinkes y'are dead.

113

Since I left you, mine eye is in my minde,
And that which governes me to goe about
Doth part his function, and is partly blind,
Seemes seeing, but effectually is out:
For it no forme delivers to the heart
Of bird, of flowre, or shape which it doth lack,
Of his quick objects hath the minde no part,
Nor his owne vision houlds what it doth catch:
For if it see the rud'st or gentlest sight,
The most sweet-favor or deformedst creature,
The mountaine, or the sea, the day, or night:
The Croe, or Dove, it shapes them to your feature.
  Incapable of more, repleat with you,
  My most true minde thus maketh mine untrue.

13 *more, repleat* more repleat

114

Or whether doth my minde being crown'd with you
Drinke up the monarks plague this flattery?
Or whether shall I say mine eie saith true,
And that your love taught it this *Alcumie*?
To make of monsters, and things indigest,
Such cherubines as your sweet selfe resemble,
Creating every bad a perfect best
As fast as objects to his beames assemble:
Oh tis the first, tis flatry in my seeing,
And my great minde most kingly drinkes it up,
Mine eie well knowes what with his gust is greeing,
And to his pallat doth prepare the cup.
  If it be poison'd, tis the lesser sinne,
  That mine eye loves it and doth first beginne.

115

Those lines that I before have writ doe lie,
Even those that said I could not love you deerer,
Yet then my judgement knew no reason why,
My most full flame should afterwards burne cleerer.
But reckening time, whose milliond accidents
Creepe in twixt vowes, and change decrees of Kings,
Tan sacred beautie, blunt the sharp'st intents,
Divert strong mindes to th'course of altring things:
Alas why fearing of times tiranie,
Might I not then say now I love you best,
When I was certaine ore in-certainty,
Crowning the present, doubting of the rest:
  Love is a Babe, then might I not say so
  To give full growth to that which still doth grow.

116

Let me not to the marriage of true mindes
Admit impediments, love is not love
Which alters when it alteration findes,
Or bends with the remover to remove.
O no, it is an ever fixed marke
That lookes on tempests and is never shaken;
It is the star to every wandring barke,
Whose worths unknowne, although his higth be taken.
Lov's not Times foole, though rosie lips and cheeks
Within his bending sickles compasse come,
Love alters not with his breefe houres and weekes,
But beares it out even to the edge of doome:
  If this be error and upon me proved,
  I never writ, nor no man ever loved.

117

Accuse me thus, that I have scanted all,
Wherein I should your great deserts repay,
Forgot upon your dearest love to call,
Whereto al bonds do tie me day by day.
That I have frequent binne with unknown mindes,
And given to time your owne deare purchas'd right,
That I have hoysted saile to al the windes
Which should transport me farthest from your sight.
Booke both my wilfulnesse and errors downe,
And on just proofe surmise, accumilate,
Bring me within the level of your frowne,
But shoote not at me in your wakened hate:
  Since my appeale saies I did strive to proove
  The constancy and virtue of your love.

14 *love.* love

118

Like as to make our appetites more keene
With eager compounds we our pallat urge,
As to prevent our malladies unseene,
We sicken to shun sicknesse when we purge.
Even so being full of your nere cloying sweetnesse,
To bitter sawces did I frame my feeding;
And sicke of wel-fare found a kind of meetnesse,
To be diseas'd ere that there was true needing.
Thus pollicie in love t'anticipate
The ills that were not, grew to faults assured,
And brought to medicine a healthfull state
Which rancke of goodnesse would by ill be cured.
  But thence I learne and find the lesson true,
  Drugs poyson him that so fell sicke of you.

10 *were not,* were, not

119

What potions have I drunke of *Syren* teares
Distil'd from Lymbecks foule as hell within,
Applying feares to hopes, and hopes to feares,
Still loosing when I saw my selfe to win?
What wretched errors hath my heart committed,
Whilst it hath thought it selfe so blessed never?
How have mine eies out of their Spheares bene fitted
In the distraction of this madding fever?
O benefit of ill, now I find true
That better is, by evil still made better.
And ruin'd love when it is built anew
Growes fairer then at first, more strong, far greater.
  So I returne rebukt to my content,
  And gaine by ills thrise more then I have spent.

120

That you were once unkind be-friends mee now,
And for that sorrow, which I then didde feele,
Needes must I under my transgression bow,
Unlesse my Nerves were brasse or hammered steele.
For if you were by my unkindnesse shaken
As I by yours, y'have past a hell of Time,
And I a tyrant have no leasure taken
To waigh how once I suffered in your crime.
O that our night of wo might have remembred
My deepest sence, how hard true sorrow hits,
And soone to you, as you to me then tendred
The humble salve, which wounded bosomes fits!
  But that your trespasse now becomes a fee,
  Mine ransoms yours, and yours must ransome mee.

121

Tis better to be vile then vile esteemed,
When not to be, receives reproach of being,
And the just pleasure lost, which is so deemed,
Not by our feeling, but by others seeing.
For why should others false adulterat eyes
Give salutation to my sportive blood?
Or on my frailties why are frailer spies;
Which in their wils count bad what I think good?
Noe, I am that I am, and they that levell
At my abuses, reckon up their owne,
I may be straight though they them-selves be bevel;
By their rancke thoughts, my deedes must not be shown
  Unlesse this generall evill they maintaine,
  All men are bad and in their badnesse raigne.

11 *bevel;* bevel

122

Thy guift, thy tables, are within my braine
Full characterd with lasting memory,
Which shall above that idle rancke remaine
Beyond all date even to eternity.
Or at the least, so long as braine and heart
Have facultie by nature to subsist,
Til each to raz'd oblivion yeeld his part
Of thee, thy record never can be mist:
That poore retention could not so much hold,
Nor need I tallies thy deare love to skore,
Therefore to give them from me was I bold,
To trust those tables that receave thee more,
  To keepe an adjunckt to remember thee,
  Were to import forgetfulnesse in mee.

1 *Thy* TThy

123

No! Time, thou shalt not bost that I doe change,
Thy pyramyds buylt up with newer might
To me are nothing novell, nothing strange,
They are but dressings of a former sight:
Our dates are breefe, and therefor we admire,
What thou dost foyst upon us that is ould,
And rather make them borne to our desire,
Then thinke that we before have heard them tould:
Thy registers and thee I both defie,
Not wondring at the present, nor the past,
For thy records, and what we see doth lye,
Made more or les by thy continuall hast:
  This I doe vow and this shall ever be,
  I will be true dispight thy syeth and thee.

124

Yf my deare love were but the childe of state,
It might for fortunes basterd be unfathered,
As subject to times love, or to times hate,
Weeds among weeds, or flowers with flowers gatherd.
No it was buylded far from accident,
It suffers not in smilinge pomp, nor falls
Under the blow of thralled discontent,
Whereto th'inviting time our fashion calls:
It feares not policy that *Heriticke,*
Which workes on leases of short numbred howers,
But all alone stands hugely pollitick,
That it nor growes with heat, nor drownes with showres.
  To this I witnes call the foles of time,
  Which die for goodnes, who have liv'd for crime.

125

Wer't ought to me I bore the canopy,
With my extern the outward honoring,
Or layd great bases for eternity,
Which proves more short then wast or ruining?
Have I not seene dwellers on forme and favor
Lose all, and more by paying too much rent
For compound sweet; Forgoing simple savor,
Pittifull thrivors in their gazing spent.
Noe, let me be obsequious in thy heart,
And take thou my oblacion, poore but free,
Which is not mixt with seconds, knows no art,
But mutuall render, onely me for thee.
  Hence, thou subbornd *Informer,* a trew soule
  When most impeacht, stands least in thy controule.

126

O thou my lovely Boy who in thy power,
Doest hould times fickle glasse, his sickle, hower:
Who hast by wayning growne, and therein shou'st,
Thy lovers withering, as thy sweet selfe grow'st.
If Nature (soveraine misteres over wrack)
As thou goest onwards still will plucke thee backe,
She keepes thee to this purpose, that her skill
May time disgrace, and wretched mynuits kill.
Yet feare her O thou minnion of her pleasure,
She may detaine, but not still keepe her tresure !
  Her *Audite* (though delayd) answer'd must be,
  And her *Quietus* is to render thee.

7 *skill* skill. 8 *mynuits* mynuit

127

In the ould age blacke was not counted faire,
Or if it weare it bore not beauties name
But now is blacke beauties successive heire,
And Beautie slanderd with a bastard shame,
For since each hand hath put on Natures power,
Fairing the foule with Arts faulse borrow'd face,
Sweet beauty hath no name no holy boure,
But is prophan'd, if not lives in disgrace.
Therefore my Mistresse eyes are Raven blacke,
Her hairs so suted, and they mourners seeme,
At such who not borne faire no beauty lack,
Slandring Creation with a false esteeme,
  Yet so they mourne becomming of their woe,
  That every toung saies beauty should looke so.

10 *hairs* eyes

128

How oft when thou my musike musike playst,
Upon that blessed wood whose motion sounds
With thy sweet fingers when thou gently swayst,
The wiry concord that mine care confounds,
Do I envie those jackes that nimble leape,
To kisse the tender inward of thy hand,
Whilst my poore lips which should that harvest reape,
At the woods bouldnes by thee blushing stand.
To be so tikled they would change their state,
And situation with those dancing chips,
Ore whome thy fingers walke with gentle gate,
Making dead wood more blest then living lips,
  Since sausie Jackes so happy are in this,
  Give them thy fingers, me thy lips to kisse.

11 *thy* their   14 *thy* their

129

Th'expence of Spirit in a waste of shame
Is lust in action, and till action, lust
Is perjurd, murdrous, blouddy full of blame,
Savage, extreame, rude, cruell, not to trust,
Injoyd no sooner but dispised straight,
Past reason hunted, and no sooner had
Past reason hated as a swollowed bayt,
On purpose layd to make the taker mad.
Mad in pursut and in possession so,
Had, having, and in quest, to have extreame,
A blisse in proofe and prov'd a very wo,
Before a joy proposd behind a dreame,
  All this the world well knowes yet none knowes well
  To shun the heaven that leads men to this hell.

9 *Mad in* made In 11 *a very wo* and very wo

130

My Mistres eyes are nothing like the Sunne,
Currall is farre more red, then her lips red,
If snow be white, why then her brests are dun
If haires be wiers, black wiers grow on her head:
I have seene Roses damaskt, red and white,
But no such Roses see I in her cheekes,
And in some perfumes is there more delight,
Then in the breath that from my Mistres reekes.
I love to heare her speake, yet well I know,
That Musicke hath a farre more pleasing sound:
I graunt I never saw a goddesse goe,
My Mistres when shee walkes treads on the ground.
  And yet by heaven I thinke my love as rare,
  As any she beli'd with false compare.

131

Thou art as tiranous, so as thou art,
As those whose beauties proudly make them cruell;
For well thou know'st to my deare doting hart
Thou art the fairest and most precious Jewell.
Yet in good faith some say that thee behold,
Thy face hath not the power to make love grone ;
To say they erre, I dare not be so bold,
Although I sweare it to my selfe alone.
And to be sure that is not false I sweare
A thousand grones but thinking on thy face,
One on anothers necke do witnesse beare
Thy blacke is fairest in my judgements place.
  In nothing art thou blacke save in thy deeds,
  And thence this slaunder as I thinke proceeds.

132

Thine eies I love, and they as pittying me,
Knowing thy heart torment me with disdaine,
Have put on black, and loving mourners bee,
Looking with pretty ruth upon my paine.
And truly not the morning Sun of Heaven
Better becomes the gray cheeks of th'East,
Nor that full Starre that ushers in the Eaven
Doth halfe that glory to the sober West
As those two morning eyes become thy face:
O let it then as well beseeme thy heart
To mourne for me since mourning doth thee grace,
And sute thy pitty like in every part.
  Then will I sweare beauty her selfe is blacke,
  And all they foule that thy complexion lacke.

133

Beshrew that heart that makes my heart to groane
For that deepe wound it gives my friend and me;
I'st not ynough to torture me alone,
But slave to slavery my sweet'st friend must be.
Me from my selfe thy cruell eye hath taken,
And my next selfe thou harder hast ingrossed,
Of him, my selfe, and thee I am forsaken,
A torment thrice three-fold thus to be crossed:
Prison my heart in thy steele bosomes warde,
But then my friends heart let my poore heart bale,
Who ere keepes me, let my heart be his garde,
Thou canst not then use rigor in my Jaile.
  And yet thou wilt, for I being pent in thee,
  Perforce am thine and all that is in me.

134

So now I have confest that he is thine,
And I my selfe am morgag'd to thy will,
My selfe Ile forfeit, so that other mine,
Thou wilt restore to be my comfort still:
But thou wilt not, nor he will not be free,
For thou art covetous, and he is kinde,
He learnd but suretie-like to write for me,
Under that bond that him as fast doth binde.
The statute of thy beauty thou wilt take,
Thou usurer that put'st forth all to use,
And sue a friend, came debter for my sake,
So him I loose through my unkinde abuse.
  Him have I lost, thou hast both him and me,
  He paies the whole, and yet am I not free.

135

Who ever hath her wish, thou hast thy *Will*,
And *Will* too boote, and *Will* in over-plus,
More then enough am I that vexe thee still,
To thy sweet will making addition thus.
Wilt thou whose will is large and spatious,
Not once vouchsafe to hide my will in thine,
Shall will in others seeme right gracious,
And in my will no faire acceptance shine:
The sea all water, yet receives raine still,
And in aboundance addeth to his store,
So thou beeing rich in *Will* adde to thy *Will*,
One will of mine to make thy large *Will* more.
  Let no unkinde, no faire beseechers kill,
  Thinke all but one, and me in that one *Will*.

136

If thy soule check thee that I come so neere,
Sweare to thy blind soule that I was thy *Will*,
And will thy soule knowes is admitted there,
Thus farre for love, my love-sute sweet fullfill.
Will, will fulfill the treasure of thy love,
I fill it full with wils, and my will one,
In things of great receit with ease we proove,
Among a number one is reckon'd none.
Then in the number let me passe untold,
Though in thy stores account I one must be,
For nothing hold me, so it please thee hold,
That nothing me, a some-thing sweet to thee.
  Make but my name thy love, and love that still,
  And then thou lovest me for my name is *Will*.

137

Thou blinde foole love, what doost thou to mine eyes,
That they behold and see not what they see:
They know what beautie is, see where it lyes,
Yet what the best is, take the worst to be.
If eyes corrupt by over-partiall lookes,
Be anchord in the baye where all men ride,
Why of eyes falsehood hast thou forged hookes,
Whereto the judgement of my heart is tide?
Why should my heart thinke that a severall plot,
Which my heart knowes the wide worlds common place?
Or mine eyes seeing this, say this is not
To put faire truth upon so foule a face,
In things right true my heart and eyes have erred,
And to this false plague are they now transferred.

138

When my love sweares that she is made of truth,
I do beleeve her though I know she lyes,
That she might thinke me some untuterd youth,
Unlearned in the worlds false subtilties.
Thus vainely thinking that she thinkes me young,
Although she knowes my dayes are past the best,
Simply I credit her false speaking tongue,
On both sides thus is simple truth suppress:
But wherefore sayes she not she is unjust?
And wherefore say not I that I am old?
O loves best habit is in seeming trust,
And age in love, loves not t'have yeares told.
  Therefore I lye with her, and she with me,
  And in our faults by lyes we flattered be.

139

O call not me to justifie the wrong,
That thy unkindnesse layes upon my heart,
Wound me not with thine eye but with thy toung,
Use power with power, and slay me not by Art,
Tell me thou lov'st else-where; but in my sight,
Deare heart forbeare to glance thine eye aside,
What needst thou wound with cunning when thy might
Is more then my ore-prest defence can bide?
Let me excuse thee, ah my love well knowes,
Her prettie lookes have been mine enemies,
And therefore from my face she turnes my foes,
That they else-where might dart their injuries:
  Yet do not so, but since I am neere slaine,
  Kill me out-right with lookes, and rid my paine.

140

Be wise as thou art cruell, do not presse
My toung-tide patience with too much disdaine:
Least sorrow lend me words and words expresse,
The manner of my pittie wanting paine.
If I might teach thee witte better it weare,
Though not to love, yet love to tell me so,
As testie sick-men when their deaths be neere,
No newes but health from their Phisitions know.
For if I should dispaire I should grow madde,
And in my madnesse might speake ill of thee,
Now this ill wresting world is growne so bad,
Madde slanderers by madde eares beleeved be.
  That I may not be so, nor thou belyde,
  Beare thine eyes straight, though thy proud heart goe wide.

13 *belyde* be lyde

141

In faith I doe not love thee with mine eyes,
For they in thee a thousand errors note,
But 'tis my heart that loves what they dispise,
Who in dispight of view is pleasd to dote.
Nor are mine eares with thy toungs tune delighted,
Nor tender feeling to base touches prone,
Nor taste, nor smell, desire to be invited
To any sensuall feast with thee alone
But my five wits, nor my five sences can
Diswade one foolish heart from serving thee,
Who leaves unswai'd the likenesse of a man,
Thy proud hearts slave and vassall wretch to be:
  Onely my plague thus farre I count my gaine,
  That she that makes me sinne, awards me paine.

142

Love is my sinne, and thy deare vertue hate,
Hate of my sinne, grounded on sinfull loving,
O but with mine, compare thou thine owne state,
And thou shalt finde it merrits not reprooving,
Or if it do, not from those lips of thine,
That have prophan'd their scarlet ornaments,
And seald false bonds of love as oft as mine,
Robd others beds revenues of their rents.
Be it lawfull I love thee as thou lov'st those,
Whome thine eyes wooe as mine importune thee,
Roote pittie in thy heart that when it growes,
Thy pitty may deserve to pittied bee.
  If thou doost seeke to have what thou doost hide,
  By selfe example mai'st thou be denide.

143

Loe as a carefull huswife runnes to catch,
One of her fethered creatures broake away,
Sets downe her babe and makes all swift dispatch
In pursuit of the thing she would have stay:
Whilst her neglected child holds her in chace,
Cries to catch her whose busie care is bent,
To follow that which flies before her face:
Not prizing her Poore infants discontent;
So runst thou after that which flies from thee,
Whilst I thy babe chace thee a farre behind,
But if thou catch thy hope turne back to me:
And play the mothers part kisse me, be kind.
  So will I pray that thou maist have thy *Will*,
  If thou turne back and my loude crying still.

144

Two loves I have of comfort and dispaire,
Which like two spirits do sugiest me still,
The better angell is a man right faire:
The worser spirit a woman collour'd il.
To win me soone to hell my femall evill,
Tempteth my better angel from my side,
And would corrupt my saint to be a divel:
Wooing his purity with her fowle pride.
And whether that my angel be turn'd finde,
Suspect I may, yet not directly tell,
But being both from me both to each friend,
I gesse one angel in an others hel.
  Yet this shal I nere know but live in doubt,
  Till my bad angel fire my good one out.

6 *side* sight

145

Those lips that Loves owne hand did make,
Breath'd forth the sound that said I hate,
To me that languisht for her sake:
But when she saw my wofull state,
Straight in her heart did mercie come,
Chiding that tongue that ever sweet,
Was usde in giving gentle dome:
And tought it thus a new to greete:
I hate she alterd with an end,
That follow'd it as gentle day,
Doth follow night who like a fiend
From heaven to hell is flowne away.
  I hate, from hate away she threw,
  And sav'd my life saying not you.

146

Poore soule the center of my sinfull earth,
Gull'd by these rebbell powres that thee array,
Why dost thou pine within and suffer dearth
Painting thy outward walls so costlie gay?
Why so large cost having so short a lease,
Dost thou upon thy fading mansion spend?
Shall wormes inheritors of this excesse
Eate up thy charge? is this thy bodies end?
Then soule live thou upon thy servants losse,
And let that pine to aggravat thy store;
Buy tearmes divine in selling houres of drosse:
Within be fed, without be rich no more,
  So shalt thou feed on death, that feeds on men,
  And death once dead, ther's no more dying then.

2 *Gull'd by* My sinfull earth

147

My love is as a feaver longing still,
For that which longer nurseth the disease,
Feeding on that which doth preserve the ill,
Th'uncertaine sicklie appetite to please:
My reason the Phisition to my love,
Angry that his prescriptions are not kept
Hath left me, and I desperate now approove,
Desire is death, which Phisick did except.
Past cure I am, now Reason is past care,
And frantick madde with ever-more unrest,
My thoughts and my discourse as mad mens are.
At randon from the truth vainely exprest.
  For I have sworne thee faire, and thought thee bright,
  Who art as black as hell, as darke as night.

148

O me! what eyes hath love put in my head,
Which have no correspondence with true sight,
Or if they have, where is my judgment fled,
That censures falsely what they see aright?
If that be faire whereon my false eyes dote,
What meanes the world to say it is not so?
If it be not, then love doth well denote,
Loves eye is not so true as all mens: no,
How can it? O how can loves eye be true,
That is so vext with watching and with teares?
No marvaile then though I mistake my view,
The sunne it selfe sees not, till heaven cleeres.
  O cunning love, with teares thou keepst me blinde,
  Least eyes well seeing thy foule faults should finde.

149

Canst thou O cruell, say I love thee not,
When I against my selfe with thee pertake:
Doe I not thinke on thee when I forgot
Am of my selfe, all tirant for thy sake?
Who hateth thee that I doe call my friend,
On whom froun'st thou that I doe faune upon,
Nay if thou lowrst on me doe I not spend
Revenge upon my selfe with present mone?
What merrit do I in my selfe respect,
That is so proude thy service to dispise,
When all my best doth worship thy defect,
Commanded by the motion of thine eyes.
  But love hate on for now I know thy minde,
  Those that can see thou lov'st, and I am blind.

150

Oh from what powre hast thou this powrefull might,
With insufficiency my heart to sway,
To make me give the lie to my true sight,
And swere that brightnesse doth not grace the day?
Whence hast thou this becomming of things il,
That in the very refuse of thy deeds,
There is such strength and warrantise of skill,
That in my minde thy worst all best exceeds?
Who taught thee how to make me love thee more,
The more I heare and see just cause of hate,
Oh though I love what others doe abhor,
With others thou shouldst not abhor my state.
  If thy unworthinesse raisd love in me,
  More worthy I to be belov'd of thee.

151

Love is too young to know what conscience is,
Yet who knowes not conscience is borne of love,
Then gentle cheater urge not my amisse,
Least guilty of my faults thy sweet selfe prove.
For thou betraying me, I doe betray
My nobler part to my grose bodies treason,
My soule doth tell my body that he may,
Triumph in love, flesh staies no farther reason,
But rysing at thy name doth point out thee,
As his triumphant prize, proud of this pride,
He is contented thy poore drudge to be
To stand in thy affaires, fall by thy side.
No want of conscience hold it that I call,
Her love, for whose deare love I rise and fall.

152

In loving thee thou know'st I am forsworne,
But thou art twice forsworne to me love swearing,
In act thy bed-vow broake and new faith torne,
In vowing new hate after new love bearing:
But why of two othes breach doe I accuse thee,
When I breake twenty: I am perjur'd most,
For all my vowes are othes but to misuse thee:
And all my honest faith in thee is lost.
For I have sworne deepe othes of thy deepe kindnesse:
Othes of thy love, thy truth, thy constancie,
And to inlighten thee gave eyes to blindnesse,
Or made them swere against the thing they see.
For I have sworne thee faire: more perjurde eye,
To swere against the truth so foule a lie.

153

Cupid laid by his brand and fell a sleepe,
A maide of *Dyans* this advantage found,
And his love-kindling fire did quickly steepe
In a could vallie-fountaine of that ground:
Which borrowd from this holie fire of love,
A datelesse lively heat still to indure,
And grew a seething bath which yet men prove,
Against strang malladies a soveraigne cure:
But at my mistres eie loves brand new fired,
The boy for triall needes would touch my brest,
I sick withall the helpe of bath desired,
And thether hied a sad distemperd guest.
  But found no cure, the bath for my helpe lies,
  Where *Cupid* got new fire; my mistres eye.

154

The little Love-God lying once a sleepe,
Laid by his side his heart inflaming brand,
Whilst many Nymphes that vou'd chast life to keep,
Came tripping by, but in her maiden hand,
The fayrest votary tooke up that fire,
Which many Legions of true hearts had warm'd,
And so the Generall of hot desire,
Was sleeping by a Virgin hand disarm'd.
This brand she quenched in a coole Well by,
Which from loves fire tooke heat perpetuall,
Growing a bath and healthfull remedy,
For men diseasd, but I my Mistrisse thrall,
  Came there for cure and this by that I prove,
  Loves fire heates water, water cooles not love.

SELECT BIBLIOGRAPHY

Editions and Texts

The *New Variorum* edition, 2 vols. ed. Hyder E. Rollins: Philadelphia, J. B. Lippincott, 1944 ed. George Wyndham (with the *Poems)*: Methuen, 1898

ed. C. K. Pooler: the *Arden* Shakespeare: Methuen (1918) 1931

ed. T. G. Tucker: Cambridge University Press, 1924

ed. G. B. Harrison (with *A Lover's Complaint*): Penguin Books, 1938

ed. C. F. Tucker Brooke: New Haven; New York, Yale University Press, 1936

Other Works

Bray, Sir Denys: *The Original Order of Shakespeare's Sonnets*: Methuen, 1925; *Shakespeare's Sonnet-Sequence*: Richards Press, 1938

Butler, Samuel: *Shakespeare's Sonnets Reconsidered and In Part Rearranged* (with the 1609 text): Longmans, 1899; new edition: Jonathan Cape, 1927

Chambers, Sir Edmund: *William Shakespeare*: *a study of facts and problems*: 2 vols., Oxford University Press, 1930

Empson, William: *Seven Types of Ambiguity*: Chatto (1930) 1947; *Some Versions of Pastoral*: Chatto (1935) 1950

Hotson, Leslie: *Shakespeare's Sonnets Dated*: Hart-Davis, 1949

Hubler, Edward: *The Sense* of *Shakespeare's Sonnets*: Princeton, 1952

Knight, G. Wilson: *The Mutual Flame*: Methuen, 1955

Onions, C. T.: *A Shakespeare Glossary*: Oxford University Press (1911) 1953

Ransom, John Crowe: *The World's Body*: Scribners, 1938

Shakespeare's England: an account of the life and manners of his age: 2 vols. Oxford University Press, 1916

Simpson, Percy: *Shakespearian Punctuation*: Oxford, Clarendon Press, 1911

COMMENTARY

For a discussion of 1-17 see Introduction (pp.31-34)

1

2. *That*: 'so that', as often elsewhere. *Rose*: the capitalization and italics are possibly purely compositorial; if not, then *Rose* here may stand for the neo-Platonic *Idea* (the title of Drayton's sonnet-sequence): the 'Eternal Type' of Beauty and Truth. Both Shakespeare and his readers would have been familiar with this notion.
3. *riper*: older.
5-7. 'You are feeding on the sight of yourself, and thus consuming yourself.' *Selfe... fewell*: fuel constituted of your own substance.
11. *content*: (i) that which you contain (your ability to procreate); (ii) your ideal happiness, which would arise from (i): i.e. your proper contentment.
12. *tender chorle*: sweet fool.
14. 'To deprive the world of your beauty by self-love; not only because death must take its course (the grave), but also by your wilful selfishness (thee).'

2

1. *fortie*: often used for an indefinite number by the Elizabethans.
3. *livery*: outward appearance.
4. *totter'd*: tattered. *weed*: a pun on the use of the word in Elizabethan English to mean 'garment'.
8. *thriftlesse*: profitless.
9. *deserv'd*: would have deserved. *use*: here means 'investment', continuing the sense of 'thriftlesse', but with a pun on the sexual connotation.
10-12. *this . . . thine*: editors end speech beginning 'this' at 'excuse'; I take it to end at 'thine', referring to the world, whose 'due' the Friend's hypothetical child would be, and to whom this hypothetical and rhetorical answer is addressed in old age. The sense is then: 'My child vindicates me of the charge of robbing you of your due, and squares my account with you; just as I argued, when young, that I perpetuated my father's beauty, so he argues now.'

3

3. *fresh repaire*: youthfulness.
5. *un-eard*: untilled, i.e. therefore not producing fruit.
7. *so fond*: so foolish – in the sense of 'infatuated'. *tombe,*: the comma is usually omitted, but the sense (of this with 1. 8) is: 'Who is so infatuated (with himself)

that he would take upon himself the function of death ('be the tombe'), thus for the sake of self-love refusing to procreate?' To 'be the tombe' is to 'live remembred not to be' (1. 12): i.e. deliberately to keep his beauty to himself. (See 4. 13).

4

4. *franck*: bounteous.
7-8. 'Usurer who makes no profit, how is it that you can invest so huge a sum (i.e. your beauty) and yet starve (i.e. gain no interest on your investment)?'
9. *traffike*: business.
12. *Audit*: Balance-sheet; account.
14. *th'executor*: thy executor.

5

2. *gaze*: that which is gazed at.
4. *unfaire*: verb, to make no longer fair.
6. *confounds*: destroys.
7. *leav's*: This apostrophe was common in the nominative plural.
14. *Leese*: Lose.

6

1. *wragged*: rough, or perhaps roughening.
5. *use*: interest payable on borrowed money. *forbidden usery*: Although Henry VIII's law permitting usury had been revived in 1571, public opinion condemned compulsory charges of interest on debts; however, it was beginning to acquiesce in loans on previously agreed terms of interest.
6. *happies*: makes happy.
8. *ten for one*: Ten per cent was the highest interest allowable under Henry VIII's original statute.
10. *refigur'd*: represented anew.

7

A comparison of the sun's diurnal course with the life of the Friend.
2. *each . . . eye*: each eye beneath the sun.
5. *steepe . . . hill*: steep up-towards-heaven (i.e. high) hill.
9. *wery car*: an allusion to Phoebus and his chariot.
11. *fore*: before.
14. *get*: beget.

8

1. 'Why do you, whose voice is music to hear, listen to music morosely?'
3-4. 'Either you love music but hate listening to it, or you dislike it but enjoy the sound of it.'
7-8. *confounds . . . beare*: 'you destroy, by remaining unmarried, the harmony that nature intended you to enjoy.' (The strings of a lute were tuned in pairs, except the highest, which was single.)
9-10. *marke . . . each*: when only one string is struck the companion string of the same pitch resounds sympathetically.
14. *thou . . . none*: The sonnet depends, rather precariously, upon the figure of the Friend as the single string.

9

4. *makelesse*: widowed.
5. *still*: always; for ever.
7. *every . . . widdow*: every individual widow.
10. *his*: refers to what the unthrift spends.
14. *murdrous shame*: shameful murder.

10

6. *stickst not*: *you* do not scruple.
9. *thought*: attitude. *minde*: opinion.

11

2. *from . . . departest*: 'you will grow (in your child) from what you leave behind (i.e. your beauty)'.
3. *yongly*: early in life.
4. *when . . . convertest*: when you change from youth to middle or old age.
11. 'To whomever nature has been most liberal, she has been more than liberal to you.' (Looke whom = whomever.)
12. *in bounty*: by being prolific.

12

4. *sable . . . white*: This is usually emended to 'all silver'd o'er'. However, it probably means 'the golden tints in black hair silvered over with white.' Or: the tincture of gold in armorial bearings, here used figuratively. *Ore*: old form of 'o'er'.

6. *erst*: formerly.
7. *girded up*: tied securely.
13. *sieth*: scythe.
14. *breed*: offspring.

13

1. ... *selfe*: the sense is: 'O that you were yourself unchangeably', i.e. Shakespeare wishes that the Friend 'owned' himself in the sense that he possessed the power to resist the changes wrought by time.
1-2. *but... live*: 'but you retain your personal identity (with which, Shakespeare implies, you are so much in love) only as long as you live'. (Then = than.)
6. *determination*: end.

14

1. *plucke*: obtain.
2. *Astronomy*: astrology; here, literally, 'astrological ability'.
6. *Pointing*: appointing
8. *By oft predict*: by frequent prediction.
14. *date*: end.

15

4. *secret . . . comment*: 'Influence' was an astrological term. The stars are compared to the spectators at a play; their control of the destiny of the players is secret and unnoticed.
5-6. The fortunes of men are no less pre-determined than those of plants. But 'selfe-same skie' also refers to the 'Stars' of l. 4: 'Cheared and checkt' carries not only the sense of 'their growth alternatively encouraged and retarded' but also, ironically, that of spectators who cheer on the players while secretly arranging and looking forward to their doom.
8. *were . . . memory*: until their beauty is entirely forgotten.
9. 'Then this notion of Nature's mutability...'
14. *ingraft*: engrave, i.e. celebrate your loveliness in my poetry.

16

6. *unset*: unsown.
8. *much liker*: much more like you. *painted counterfeit*: portrait.
9. *the . . . life*: living lines: i.e. drawn by Nature, as opposed to those of a portrait, or the lines of Shakespeare's poems (cf. l. 4). There is also a play on the 'line of

life' in palmistry: this is supposed to reveal prospects of marriage and children. *repaire*: preserve.
10. *this (Times . . . pen)*: The parenthesis refers to 'this'. *Times pensel*: refers to the painted counterfeit of l. 8; *my pupill pen*: this has been taken as evidence that Sonnets 1-17 are amongst Shakespeare's earliest work, but the sense is 'my pen, the pupil of your beauty; just as the artist's hand is guided by your beauty'. The 'pensel' (which may have denoted a portrait-artist's small brush) belongs to 'Time' because Shakespeare is arguing that only by procreation may the Friend preserve his beauty in the face of Time's tyranny: the Friend's vanity, his contentment with his portrait (and with Shakespeare's complimentary verses, no doubt), is equally the property of Time.
11. *faire*: beauty.

17

4. *parts*: good qualities.
6. *fresh numbers*: new poems.
11. *true rights*: the praises that are due to you. Poets rage: Poet's exaggerated passion.
12. *miter*: metre.
14. *twise*: twice. *rime*: poetry.

18

3. *Maie*: May ended only a few days before midsummer in the Elizabethan Calendar.
7-8. 'In time all beautiful things lose their beauty, whether by some accident, or in the course of nature.' *untrim'd*: divested of ornament.
10. *loose*: lose. *ow'st*: possessest.
12. *grow'st* becomest part of.

20

This sonnet has caused much consternation among commentators owing to its alleged indecency. Comments vary from Richardson s 'I could heartily wish that Shakespeare had never written it' (1840) to Rollins's 'filthy' (1944). But prudishness, fear of reality and censoriousness, rather than the sonnet, seem responsible for the perplexity which it has aroused. Shakespeare is not by habit a homosexual, he appears to say in lines 11-12, and therefore is unable to consummate his passion by the means available to homosexuals; yet his love for the Friend is greater than his love for a woman could be (lines 3-5). Although the Friend has a woman's gentleness, he lacks her falseness. What Shakespeare is

saying is that although this love has the depth of friendship between men – a depth achieved by the absence of sexual confusion – physical desire has been incited in him by the young man's womanish beauty. The sexual attractiveness of the Friend is attributed, here and elsewhere, to his feminine characteristics. The situation here revealed is not as unfamiliar in life as it is rare in poetry. A 'normally' adjusted man often discovers, to his consternation and shame, that his friendship for a 'lovely boy' has deepened into a love in which sexuality, though at first it may be ecstatically eschewed, plays an increasingly dominant part. What such a man's instinct feels it is 'unlawful' to regard in the light of sensual desire (the 'one thing' added by 'dotinge nature') becomes, perhaps, a symbol of the possible unselfishness that may be achieved by this love. Hence the emotion of generosity which overflows into the sonnet's final couplet, with its brilliant and poetic pun on 'prickt'. (The rather more frivolous sense of 42 shows how soon this kind of emotion can weaken and degenerate.)
2. *Master Mistris*: Most editors supply a hyphen, but the text allows 'Master Mistris' as a secondary meaning; the subtler primary sense is: 'one who fulfils the function of a mistress, but is superior to one in that, because male, he *masters* my passion'. *passion*: 'ardent love'; also, perhaps, 'love-poetry'.
6. 'Making the objects you look upon beautiful' (and, perhaps, good).
7. *Hews*: It is doubtful whether, as C. J. Sisson suggests in his *New Readings*, the italics are 'purely compositorial'. The existence of someone called Hews need not lead us to the conclusion that this was the Friend: some third person is probably referred to, in a private joke. (See Introduction, pp. 15-16.)
8. *Which*: refers to 'his controwling'. *steales*: There is a pun here: (i) attracts the gazes of all men, by stealing them from women; (ii) *steels* the gazes of men, so that they do not look desirously. (A reference, in one word, to the Friend's sexual attractiveness and to his spiritual power to subdue lust.)
11. *defeated*: defrauded.
13. *prickt*: (i) selected; (ii) endowed with a prick (= penis). Cf. *2 Henry IV, III, ii,* 122-125: 'I was pricked well enough before, an you could have left me alone. My old dame will be undone now for one to do her husbandry and her drudgery…'
14. *use*: sexual use.

21

This may easily be read as an attack, partly in the form of a parody, on Daniel, Constable, Watson or even Sidney, all of whose sonnets are full of such conceits. Even Chapman may be intended; see 13-14 below.
4. *reherse*: literally, 'mention'; here it seems to mean 'compare'.
8. *rondure*: roundness: the circumference of the horizon. A fanciful term perhaps deliberately reminiscent of Chapman in *The Shadow of Night.*
12. *gould candells*: the stars.

13-14. 'Let those who rely on mere hearsay continue to write in this vein; I shall not indulge in such vulgar salesmanship, since I do not desire to part with my beloved': i.e. Shakespeare is not in love half-heartedly, and with an eye to the main chance. If 'purpose' is read as a noun, 1. 14 emerges as a very ironic aside: 'Certainly I shall never feel like making false analogies such as I have been describing about *that*!' It has been suggested that there is a play on Chapman's name here, since 'purpose not to sell' means 'not to be a *Chapman*'.

22

3. *forrwes*: furrows.
4. *expiate*: end.
8. *elder*: older.

23

1. *unperfect*: not fully versed in his part.
3-4. 'Like a wild beast whose violent rage undermines its own strength.' 'Rage' also here means 'lust', giving the sense of: 'Like one made impotent by too much lust'. Cf. lines 7-8.
5-6. Being a lover, Shakespeare has a part to play, like an actor; but he forgets it (i) in fear of the sort of reception he will get, (ii) in diffidence. 'Trust, is used in both an active and a passive sense to convey the double meaning; but there is also a play on the legal sense: his physical desire is held *in trust*; he is afraid of abusing it by saying too much. *perfect... right*: (i) the declaration of love natural to a lover; (ii) physical sexual relationship. There is a play on 'rite', but no need to bring it into the text, as most editors have done.
7-8. Hints at the practical difficulties of such a love.
9. Shakespeare is attempting to rationalize a situation that is impossible in practice: to give validity to an impossible love by expressing it in poetic terms. 11. *Who pleade*: refers to 'books' and 'domb presagers', not to 'speaking brest'.
13-14. This is nothing less than an invocation to the Friend to understand Shakespeare's poetic purpose. 'Silent love' would write the truth, since it could seek no lustful gain. 'To heare with eies' is an apt description of reading poetry.

24

Miss M. M. Mahood says of this confused sonnet: 'The resultant image is pure Bosch.' It may briefly be summarized thus: 'My eye (as painter) has drawn a picture of you on my heart; my heart is held by (i.e. is in) my frame, and perspective is the highest skill of the painter. (There is a play on 'frame': (i) corporeal frame (ii) perspective (iii) frame of a picture.) It is through the painter (i.e. my eyes, which have drawn your picture) that you may discover my depiction of your spiritual beauty hanging in the frame of my body, as in a shop whose windows are your eyes – thus have we exchanged eyes, and see what a bargain it has proved to be! My eyes have recorded your picture (i.e. as painter: they drew it), while your eyes are windows in my breast, through which the sun loves to shine in order to behold you. Yet eyes ((i) the image of you, (ii) the painter) require wisdom to know the beauty of the heart as well as of what they see.'

25

4. *unlookt for*: inconspicuously.
9. *painefull*: toilsome. *worth*: Shakespeare probably meant to write 'fight' or 'might' here; there is no reason to blame the mistake on the compositor.

26

While this sonnet does not prove that Southampton was the Friend (see Introduction, p. 17), it is difficult to suppose that it could have been written to a person of even similar social status to Shakespeare's, or to anyone below it.
3. *written ambassage*: message conveyed by an ambassador. This almost certainly refers to the sonnet itself.
5-8. 'I trust that your esteemed reading of my poor lines will infuse some body and meaning into them.'
9. *moving*: destiny, actions.
10. 'Casts a benign influence upon me.'
11. *tottered*: See 2. 4, n.
13-14. 'I will await better fortune before I put myself in a position where you could test my devotion to you.'

27

1. *toyle*: the weariness of travel.
2. *travaill*: work.
4. *worke*: stimulate.
6. *intend*: set out upon.
8. 'Seeing no more than the blind see.'
10. *shaddoe*: ghost; here, 'phantasm of the living'.

28

A sequel to, and comment upon, 27.
5. *ethers*: each other's.

6. 'Agree to unite to torture me.'
9. The speech to Day may begin at 'to' or 'thou', according to whether 'him' refers to the Friend or to the day.
10. 'Your presence makes a cloudy day seem bright.'
12. *twire*: peep. *guil'st th'eaven*: 'Make the sky look as though the sun were shining.'
13-14. Editors usually transpose 'longer' and 'stronger', or emend 'length' to' 'strength'. The sense of Q, however, is: 'The day's journey takes me away from you and causes me to think of the intolerable duration of my sorrow at our separation; and at night, when I dwell upon this, it appears to be even more permanent.'

29

3. *bootlesse*: useless.
6. *like... him*: like this one, like that one.
7. *art*: talent, craftsmanship. *skope*: range of skill.
8. Probably a reference to Shakespeare's poetry.
12. *sullen*: gloomy.

30

1-2. The legal metaphor, unobtrusive though it is, adds the notion of guilt and punishment to that of nostalgia. 'And I mourn again the precious time I have wasted in seeking for what I did not find.'
6. *dateles*: endless.
8. *sight*: sigh. The line means: 'lament the sighs of grief that wasted me long ago'. There was an old belief that sighing impaired the health.
9. *fore-gon*: gone before.
10. *tell*: count.
11. *fore-bemoned*: already lamented.

31

1. *indeared*: made more precious.
5. *obsequious*: dutiful with regard to death.
6. *religious*: faithful – again, with regard to the dead.
7. *interest*: right. *which*: who.
8. *there*: refers to 'bosome' (l. 1).
11. *parts*: shares (what love I gave them).
12. *That*: used relatively.
14. *all they*: you who combine all their qualities.

32

1. *well contented daie*: the day of my death, with which I shall be well-contented.
2. *churle death*: that rude fellow, Death.
4. As Empson writes, 'Line 4 is isolated between colons, and is the pivot around which the rest of the sonnet turns...' *poore rude lines*: doubtless Shakespeare had been taunted with lack of style. and had been nettled by it.
5. *bett'ring of the time*: a time in which poets are getting better – at least so far as their style is concerned.
7. *Reserve*: Preserve. The line means: 'Preserve them for their content, not for their accomplishment'.
8. *happier men*: (i) men who are happier in their emotional relationships than I; (ii) men whose verse is more felicitous than mine.
9-14. It is clear that Shakespeare, though less learned than perhaps the majority of contemporary writers, and almost certainly acutely aware of this, nevertheless deprecated the emphasis they put on learning. He felt about it in critical as well as envious terms. He implies here that he wishes he were learned; but the inference is inescapable: discerning people are never going to read a stylist in preference to a lover.

33

Here Shakespeare intends, as John Crowe Ransom remarks in *The World's Body,* 'an all-ruling fair-weather sun to be the symbol of his false friend...' It is the sun, the Friend, that is obscured.
2. *soveraine eie*: The sun is compared to a King whose gaze flatters everyone on whom it rests.
5. *basest*: darkest; also, 'morally lowest; most disgusting'.
6. *rack*: the floating motion of the clouds.
12. *region cloude*: the clouds above.
13-14. 'Him' refers to 'region cloude'. The Friend does not acknowledge the 'disgrace' (in which he is in fact as much implicated as Shakespeare) as such. The final line gives Shakespeare's own reason for his beloved's look of disdain if the sun itself grows dim, then even the best people do also. The main sense is that Shakespeare now accepts that his is no ideal love, as he had perhaps supposed. 'Staine' and 'staineth' are intransitive, and mean 'grow dim', 'become obscured', or, possibly, 'lose colour'.

34

Closely linked with the preceding. The identification of the Friend with the sun is continued. At first reading it may appear that Shakespeare feels himself disgraced: that whatever disservice his friend has done him has caused him to feel guilt. And so the sonnet has been read. To some extent this is correct (see Introduction, pp. 29 and 34-35) but a close study of the text (and of 33) will not support this interpretation as the primary meaning. All editors since Malone (following Capell) have abetted it by reading 'cross' for 'losse' in l. 12; but it seems to me that the text of Q must stand: the repetition may be a mistake, but it is more likely to have been an effective 'Freudian slip' on Shakespeare's part than on that of the printer. What he means when he implies that he has been robbed by the 'disgrace' of the 'strong offense' is that his idealistic picture of his beloved has been shattered. We know from 33 that the Friend himself is indifferent to the 'disgrace', but that Shakespeare, on the contrary, has been deeply grieved by it. In other words, Shakespeare's view of the Friend has been robbed ('beares the strong offenses losse') by the corruption ('staine') revealed in him. The Friend's 'shame', since he has not discernment enough to see the 'region cloude', must represent no more than an ordinary desire to make amends, to avoid fuss: it 'lends but weake reliefe'. Shakespeare reveals that now he understands that to love truly he must suffer *for* his friend when he plays him false, as well as on his own account. The 'griefe' here is primarily not for his own disgrace, but for his friend's; and his friend's shame can give no 'phisicke' for it because Shakespeare realizes its superficial nature. Lines 5-12 explain that it is not enough that the sun has come out again: he cannot accept that the Friend is what he was before. He understands that 'suns of the world may staine'. He recognizes his tears of repentance for what they are; but he also recognizes that it is the Friend's love for him, whatever this is worth, which has shed them. They are the best he can show and do not at all resemble the idealized sun which came out to dry his own 'storme-beaten face': what they do resemble is the stormy baseness of his true nature. And, being true (whatever that implies), being understood, being recognized, they are 'pearle'; poetic understanding releases the generosity of forgiveness. In the final couplet the image of the Friend's tears recollects the sudden treachery of the very 'storm' which overtook Shakespeare.

2. *travaile*: travel.

4. *brav'ry*: splendour.

8. *heales*: Tucker (ed. 1924) read 'heles', meaning 'hides'. It is more likely that Shakespeare means that the Friend's false repentance, his readiness to resume the relationship on the old terms, is merely an ointment which, while it can easily heal the wounded feelings which Shakespeare has sustained, cannot change the Friend's nature. *cures... disgrace*: does not obliterate the scar.

13. *sheeds*: sheds.

35

6. Shakespeare has done this in 33, 14.

7. Corrupting myself by excusing your evil action.
8. 'Make your sins seem greater by excusing them with a vehemence far greater than they deserve.'
9. Explains why Shakespeare corrupts himself, and why he magnifies the Friend's sins: 'I bring in my intellectual condemnations and justifications to a wrong action of yours which was wholly impelled by sensuality'.
10. 'And against myself I enter a justifiable plea.'
11. Shakespeare enters the plea because there is a conflict between his love for the Friend and his hatred of the 'sensuall fault'. Although the case against himself is based on the fact that the 'civill war' involves a betrayal, the legal metaphor reveals that the matter can be settled only by a proper trial. Shakespeare hints that he is sensually tempted, since the opposing advocate is the Friend's sensuality.
13-14. In the sense that he is pleading against himself on the grounds that his 'hate' represents a betrayal, Shakespeare is recognizing that the circumstances have now forced him to give comfort to that very sensuality which detracts from his love. But in personal terms, exclusive of the Friend, he is pleading against himself because of his *own* sensuality: he is giving comfort to the 'sweet' motives of idealistic friendship, which must, in these new circumstances, rob him of everything.

36

A temporary solution to the problem of 35: Shakespeare acknowledges that the sensual side of himself has won. Therefore they can never meet again.
1-2. The sonorous opening 'Let me confesse' gives the clue to the theme. 'Although we desire the same thing, we must remain apart.'
3-4. 'Only in this way can my "blot" (sensual desire for you, as well as the public disgrace of 34) be overcome: your help would make this intolerable.'
5. *one respect*: 'one thing we both look to': i.e. our desire for each other.
6. *seperable spight*: Undoubtedly the element of sensuality which has entered into their relationship is referred to.
8. 'We cannot spend time in one another's company, since we should make love to one another (and this we cannot do).'

37

3. There is no reason to suppose, with Butler, that this 'lameness' is literal; 36 tells us how Shakespeare feels that he has been morally crippled by circumstance.
4. By loving the Friend at a distance, Shakespeare can preserve in him all the qualities of 'worth and truth' that he has lost.
7. *Intitled in their parts*: entitled to their positions in this hierarchy.
8. *ingrafted*: firmly fixed, rooted. Broadly the line means that Shakespeare will

dedicate his love to the perpetuation of the virtues of the Friend.
10. *that*: refers to 'this store'. *this shadow*: myself, in my separate and unhappy condition.
11. This line states the only way in which Shakespeare can properly live; it does not mean, of course, that he is doing so.

38

2. *that*: refers to 'thou'. *poor'st*: pourest.
3. *argument*: theme, subject.
3-4. *to... rehearse*: 'too good to serve as a theme for ordinary verse'.
5-6. 'Thank yourself for any worthy lines you may find in my poems'.
13. *curious*: accurate, demanding.
14. *paine*: work, with a play on the sense of 'suffering'.

39

1. *with manners*: not unbecomingly.
5-8. 'Let us live separately for the sake of this (my being able to praise you without praising myself) and let our singleness lose its public notoriety, so that I may be able to award you the praise which only you (and not I) deserve'. *give*: the colon emphasizes the next line.

40

It emerges clearly from this and the two following sonnets, precise biographical considerations apart, that the Friend has successfully supplanted Shakespeare in the affections of a woman.
1-4. 'You have nothing more than you had before if you fall in love with someone whom I have truly loved, because everything I have possessed was yours even before you possessed it.'
5-6. 'I cannot blame you if you substitute love for my mistress for your love for me: my love being yours, it is my love you are using (see 20, 14)'. There are puns, of course, on the second and third 'my love'. *usest*: (i) employ (ii) go to bed with (my mistress).
7-8. Most editors substitute 'thyselfe' for Q's 'this selfe'. But 'this' is necessary, precisely to distinguish it from 'thyselfe'. Shakespeare specifically means 'that part of you, that self, which uses my love'. He is saying: 'Yet you are to blame if you are doing this merely to spite me, if you do not mean it for its own sake'. *taste*: enjoyment.
10. *poverty*: the little I have.
11-12. 'Yet love, if nothing else, knows that it is harder to be hurt by one you

love than to be wronged publicly by an enemy.'
13-14. 'Lascivious and yet beautiful young man, guilty of all manner of malice, spite me as much as you can, yet we must not be enemies.'

41

1. *pretty*. One of the most ironically used words in the sonnets.
4. (i) You are young and easily led; (ii) you tempt people.
7-8. The man 'prevails' in the sexual sense (see 13 below), so that the usual emendation 'she' for 'he' is unnecessary and wrong. The woman wants the man to prevail.
9. *my seate forbeare*: refrain from usurping my position with her.
11. *who*: refers to 'beauty' and 'straying youth'.
13. 'By tempting her with your beauty you make her false to me. It is, however, of the essence of gallantry that a man should appear not to prevail when he might do so (see 8 above).'
14. 'By *using* your beauty, and thus being false to me.'

42

Shakespeare here makes his feelings over the loss of his mistress more strongly evident. Critics have found the 'superhuman forgiveness' evinced in it hard to accept. The metaphor of the Friend who possesses all Shakespeare's love is, however, meant to be just as difficult to accept as Shakespeare found it: he was trying to feel like this, and finding it hard going. This was not essentially a masochistic frame of mind, although it may seem so: it was a desire, made increasingly difficult by the Friend's apparently treacherous and spiteful nature, to continue to love ('we must not be foes') and at the same time to be truthful – not to indulge in false comparisons.
5-6. An artificial 'excuse', but in the light of later sonnets, and of what is hinted here in l. 12, it can be accepted even without irony. It must be noted in general that Shakespeare's tone to the Friend is becoming increasingly remote in matters of poetic argument: he is writing more introspectively and less in order to be understood.
7. 'She deceives me because she knows that you make love to her because I love you'. *abuse*: ill-treat, deceive.
8. *approove*: (i) approve of (as a convenient foil to spite Shakespeare); (ii) know her carnally.
9-10. 'She gains if I lose you, and you gain if I lose her; therefore I suffer a double loss.'
12. This line is undoubtedly ironic in relation to the Friend and the Mistress; but, like the 'excuse' of lines 5-6 above, it can also be taken without irony: it anticipates

such lines as 141, 14 – if, indeed, the 'Mistress' sequence was not written roughly contemporaneously with 40-42 (see Introduction, p. 14).
14. *flattery,*: The comma, rather than the usually substituted exclamation mark, is just right here: Shakespeare and his Friend are *not* one, and there is no 'Sweete flattery' outside Shakespeare's own imagination.

43

1. (i) When I am asleep and dreaming, I see most enjoyably (i.e. he does not see the Friend's bad character); (ii) when I seem most gullible, then I am most carefully taking things in.
2. *unrespected*: (i) unnoticed (ii) not worthy of respect – a hint that there are things about the Friend that are not worthy of respect.
4. *and darkely bright*: brightened, in sleep or in the dark inactivity of night, by my love of what they look for and at. *are... directed*: 'bright in dark' is an adverbial phrase limiting 'directed': 'thus brightened in the dark and automatically directed at you'.
6. *thy... forme*: 'the form (you) that produces your shadow (the image of you in my mind).'
6-8. 'How happy I would be to see the real you, when the mere imagination of you illumines the darkness!'
9-10. 'Would my eyes be blessed by seeing the real you?' This question reveals that Shakespeare is not sure that his introspective idealization of the Friend is not preferable to his relationship with him in reality.
11. It is imperfect because it is the image and not the real thing; but the word politely carries other implications.
13-14. A straightforwardly emotional statement in deliberate contrast to the forebodings of the preceding lines.

44

This, and the following, figuratively employ the notion that life is constituted of the two heavy elements, earth and water, and the two light elements, fire and air. The idea would have been familiar to Shakespeare and his readers from Golding's translation of Ovid's *Metamorphoses*.
2. *injurious distance*. The geographical *motif* is a metaphor for the 'seperable spight'.
4. *where... stay*: wherever you are.
9. The exercise of my intellect presents me with the devastating fact that I cannot travel to you in this way.
10. *when....gone*: at times when you are not present.
11. 'That' is synonymous with 'one'. The line means: one who is so constituted

that the heavier elements predominate. The two lines 9 and 11, taken together, suggest that Shakespeare blames his intellect for this; 1. 9 can mean: 'it is thought (intellect) that makes me worldly.'
12. There is a play on 'attend': (i) pay attention to; (ii) wait upon. The comma (usually removed) gives the first three words a necessary emphasis.
13-14. The basis of the metaphor is that tears are both watery (of water) and heavy (of earth); the basic meaning, underlying the evocation of a present state of misery, is that this state of affairs is leading to nothing.

45

1. *slight*: insubstantial.
4. *present absent*: now here, now there.
5. *quicker Elements*: fire and air: 'thought' and 'desire'.
9. Until the number of elements is made complete (by the restoration of fire and air). *lives*: life's.
10-12. The bitter meaning is: 'When I do get them back, and become myself, I merely hear of your good health and spirits.'

46

Superficially, this sonnet is based upon a figure of co-owners of a piece of land, who cannot agree, going to law to decide upon the division of it. In a deeper sense it describes the conflict between Shakespeare's love (of his heart) and desire (of his eye) for the Friend. Shakespeare leaves the problem unresolved, except that by the phraseology of the final couplet he makes it clear that this conflict is not really based on the reaction of the Friend, whose outward part is only his eyes' due, and whose 'inward love of heart' is merely Shakespeare's heart's 'right'– though not what it gets.

1. *mortall*: fatal. The existence of this conflict is fatal to Shakespeare and his love.
9. *side*: to assign to one of two parties.
10. *quest*: jury making an inquisition.
12. *moyitie*: any portion of a thing.

47

8. *his*: the heart's.

48

The underlying theme of this sonnet is the shifty and sexually coarse character of

the Friend: Shakespeare could only 'lock up' an image of him as a 'good' character in his imagination.
2. *truest*: most trustworthy. *trifle*: small valuable object; also, token, gesture of affection. The overt sense: 'so that I should be protected from the temptation of using them (each trifle, i.e. thought of you)' lends force to the true one: 'I tried to keep these shreds of you which I am able to love free from the taint of lust'. The notion of locking his own trifles away from himself has no point unless this underlying meaning be admitted.
3. *use*: 'use' frequently meant 'sexual use'.
8-10. At first this seems to indicate that Shakespeare has forgotten to 'lock up' his friend, but the implication is, of course, that he is not the sort of man who can be locked up in this way. Line 10 means both that Shakespeare has made a mistake, and that such a friend (one who could be treasured) does not exist except in Shakespeare's imagination. He only 'feels' that the Friend is in 'the gentle closure of his breast'. The sonnet means nothing if it rests on the figure of Shakespeare making a mere oversight in remembering to lock up his 'trifles', but not his friend.
9. *chest*: a play on 'coffer' and 'breast'.
12. *part*: depart.
13-14. The preceding lines have made it clear that it is an imagined image of the Friend which is 'within the gentle closure' of Shakespeare's breast; but he prophesies that he will lose even this in a final couplet, the second line of which is a piece of complex *double entendre* very characteristic of Shakespeare. He means: (i) more overtly, that such beautiful lovers are often stolen away; (ii) that, tragically, his sense of truth will assert itself against the obstinately idealized picture of his beloved. There is a play on 'deare': (i) adored (ii) hard-to-bear, grievous.

49

1. *against that time*: denotes provision made in case of a possible event.
2. 'When you will condemn my faults, rather than excuse them as a friend should.'
3. *cast... summe*: made up the final account.
4. *advis'd respects*: well-considered deliberations.
5. *strangely*: not recognizing me.
8. 'Shall find legal and ceremonious reasons for treating me thus coldly.'
9. *insconce me*: 'shelter myself in a secure position.' A sconce was an earthwork or fortification.
10. *desart*: desert, a pun, meaning both 'how poorly placed I am (in a desert) and 'lack of worth or merit'.
11-12. 'Bear witness against myself to defend your reasons for taking this attitude towards me.'

13-14. Shakespeare can show no cause why his friend should love him; but the last line simultaneously gives the bitter reason for Shakespeare's forebodings of his friend's change of attitude (also the forebodings of the concluding lines of the preceding sonnet): Shakespeare can give no reason, either, why *he* should love... He is now becoming obsessed by the corrupting nature of the person with whom he is in love; he can give no 'legal' reason (i.e. in terms of the legal metaphor used throughout the sonnet, no reason valid to Love). The underlying emotion of self-reproach is based on Shakespeare's recognition of his failure, despite his love, to transform his beloved. The experience is giving him cause to doubt the goodness of his own nature.

50

1. *heavie*: sadly.
7. *instinct*: is accented on the second syllable.
13-14. Reflects the conflict in Shakespeare's mind over his love. This is not merely an account of his feelings on a journey: the journey away from his beloved represents a difficult decision he has to make, which prudence, at least, dictates. His horse is seen as his unwilling and too-pliable conscience (cf. 151, 1). (The conscience is frequently and familiarly held to need 'spurring'.) The next sonnet develops this theme.

51

1. *slow offence*: offence of going slowly; but 'offence' – usually having the sense of 'fault', 'transgression', associated with the notion of 'disgrace', in Shakespeare – is a strong word to use here, and reinforces the identity of the horse with his conscience. The word 'love' in this and the preceding sonnet appears to be equivalent to 'desire' or 'overwhelming need for'.
2. *dull bearer*: horse. But there is a play on both words: 'dull' meaning 'physically insensible', and 'bearer' meaning 'owner' or 'possessor'. (His conscience is not vulnerable to beauty and to Shakespeare's desire for it.)
5. On the return journey his horse will have no excuse at all for slowness; another way of saying that his conscience will count for nothing.
8. 'Even if I could fly I should not seem to be moving.'
9. An acknowledgement of the beloved's absolute power over him, this line seems to state, in the terms of the deeper meaning of this sonnet, that his conscience and his love are irreconcilable.
10-14. The general meaning of these difficult lines is that Shakespeare is parting from his conscience and his better judgement, despite the warnings implicit in 48. The final couplet means: 'since my conscience was so slow to part with you, I will now dispense with it altogether'. *naigh noe dull flesh.* A famous crux,

variously emended as 'need no dull flesh', 'neigh to no dull flesh', 'weigh no dull flesh', 'wait no dull flesh', 'neigh – no dull flesh', 'neigh, no dull flesh' and 'neigh (no dull flesh)'. The last and most frequent emendation retains what is probably the correct sense of 'shall whinny with exultation like a horse, being unencumbered by the slowness of mundane travel', but the parenthesis is not necessary, and I have allowed Q to stand. There seems to be a hint that this scuttling of his conscience leaves the way open for his desire, which is no dull flesh (see 2, above), to do what it likes. *jade*: worthless, maltreated horse. Not always a term of contempt, but here it seems to be, since the horse is called a 'wretch' in 50, 7.

52

4. *For blunting*: afraid of blunting. *seldome*: used as an adjective: rare.
8. *captaine*: of greatest worth. *carconet*: a hanging collar of gold set with large jewels which were surrounded with smaller stones. Carconets were more or less confined to Court, being of very high value. One presented to Queen Elizabeth by the Earl of Warwick in the year of the Armada, made of gold, contained '15 pieces, seven sett with foure rubyes, and one small diamond in the middest, the other seven sett with nyne pearles in a piece sett in gold, having a rowe of small pearles on thupside, and pendaunt of sparks of rubyes, oppalls, and ragged pearles.'
10-12. 'Like the wardrobe in which lies hidden the most magnificent garment of some princely infant, and which has the power to make him doubly princely when it yields this garment for him to wear.'
13-14. 'You are blessed, whose worth makes it possible for me to love you in your presence, and to hope so bravely in your absence.'

53

This was described by Butler, in the spirit of his very literal interpretation, as 'a peace-offering of abundant flattery'; and many commentators have remarked on the incompatibility of the tribute with the person described in 40-42, and in others. Ostensibly a tribute, the poem is in fact a piece of direct irony; the tone of the first lines alone expresses a hurt puzzlement and the complimentary metaphor neatly conceals a far shrewder appraisal than Shakespeare's feelings will allow. His feelings are fully engaged, and have undergone no diminution, but he has not lost his poetic sense of reality which, for the moment eschewing diction and direct statement, expresses itself in tone and *double-entendre.*
1. *substance*: human substance, as contrasted with shadow, spirit; but also 'wealth', and hence, perhaps, 'success'.
2. *strange*: foreign alien to you; the use of this word is well-advised. *shaddowes*: images of beauty (here, Adonis, Helen, spring and autumn). *tend*: wait upon, as

a servant (as a literal shadow follows the person who casts it). The meaning implicit in the question, apart from the compliment, is: 'How do you manage to enslave so many people?'
3. An emphatic way of saying that each person has only one image, i.e. natural beauty.
4. 'Although you too are only one person, you can borrow the beauty of all manner of images.' There is more than a suggestion in this and the preceding lines that there is something distastefully artificial about his beloved. Shakespeare's choice of a familiar Platonic notion (that, in Lee's words, 'every beautiful aspect of nature reflects... attributes of the beloved one's form') upon which to base his conceit, is significant, in view of his probably growing lack of sympathy with Platonic artificialities. (See 21 and 32, and notes.)
5-6. 'A description of Adonis is nothing like as beautiful as you.' It should be noted that the beloved is only more beautiful than a description of Adonis, not than Adonis himself.
7-8. Can mean: 'when all beauty is added to Helen's face it resembles yours'; or, more likely, 'you resemble a painted Helen'. 'Art of beauty' may well be a reference to make-up. *tires*: head-dress; or, possibly, simply 'attire'.
9. *foyzon*: plentiful season: autumn.
13. A straightforward and sincere compliment to his beloved's beauty.
14. Ostensibly a compliment: 'no one has such constancy as you'; but the underlying meaning is: 'you feel affection for no one, and no one admires you for the virtue of constancy.'

54

2. *truth*: loyalty.
3-4. The rose was a common symbol of the Platonic idea (see 1, 2, n.), and since the preceding sonnet (see 53, 4, n.) ironically utilizes a Platonic conceit, these lines may well be intended as a direct contrast: here he speaks of a living rose, and of the true loyalty of which, as we have seen from 35, 40-42 (at least), his beloved is incapable.
5. *Canker bloomes*: dog or hedge roses.
6. *tincture*: colour; also the 'elixir of life' of the alchemists.
7. *play as wantonly*: shake playfully (in the wind).
10. *unrespected*: unlooked-on; neglected.
11-12. Perfume can be distilled from the garden-rose, whereas the dog-rose, having no scent, dies alone and benefits no one.
13. An exhortation to his beloved to emulate the superior garden-rose, not an identification of him with it. The whole sonnet is written from the standpoint of 53, but in a much less bitter mood. 11-12 are homiletic, and the couplet points the moral. *lovely*: 'amorous', not, as some editors gloss, 'lovable'.

14. *that*: 'your beauty'. *vade*: decay, perish... Frequently emended to 'fade'. *distils*: here used intransitively, with the sense of 'trickle forth', as the perfume of the crushed rose trickles forth in drops from the still.

55

Much has been written about this famous sonnet, chiefly on the subject of whether Shakespeare borrowed his theme of the triumphant immortality of his celebration of his love in verse from Horace, Ovid or from a paraphrase of Ovid in Meres's *Palladis Tamia.* It seems most likely that the source was Golding's translation of the *Metamorphoses* of Ovid, with which we know Shakespeare to have been familiar; but the point is of little importance, since this theme was commonplace and may be found in Spenser, Drayton, Daniel and others. What is more important is Shakespeare's use of it, and here John Crowe Ransom's comment (The *World's Body,* 1938) is the most pertinent: 'What it develops is not the circumstantial immortality of the rime, and of the beloved inhabiting it, but the mortality of the common marbles and monuments...' This is undoubtedly where the poetic energy comes from. As for the beloved, Ransom goes on to say: 'The only specific thing here is something about a gait'.

3. *in these contents*: in my poetry.

4. *sluttish*: A figurative use of this word, continuing the meanings 'dirty in dress and habits' and 'morally unclean'.

7. *Nor Mars his sword*: 'destroy' needs to be understood after 'sword', to parallel 'shall burne'. *burne*: the colon emphasizes 1. 8.

9. *all oblivious enmity*: everything which would cause you to be forgotten.

10. *pace forth*: become conspicuous in 'the world's eyes; but Shakespeare also used 'pace' to mean 'to train a horse', and there may be a hint of 'I shall expose you to the world in a good (i.e. changed by me, "trained") light, as someone I loved, and not as you really are'.

12. '(Posterity) who will use up (weare... out) the world until it comes to an end. This well suits the Shakespearean notion of time.

13. 'So until it is decreed by judgement that you yourself shall arise.' This line supports the intimation, already noted in 1. 10, that the real self of his beloved, as it will emerge at the judgement, is not at all the same as the person who will 'pace forth' in Shakespeare's verse. There is a suggestion here of the worthlessness of 'posterity' and 'time' in judging the beloved – almost a desperate vindication of Shakespeare's jettisoning of his conscience and better judgement; but there is also a wry acknowledgement of the final truth of the words 'so til'.

56

1. *love*: the spirit of love.
2. *edge*: keenness. *apetite*: primarily 'sexual desire', 'lust'; but also, perhaps, 'pleasure in the company of the beloved'.
3-4. Plainly a reference to the renewal of lust.
5. *love*: his beloved.
6. *winck with fulnesse*: close with drowsiness.
7-8. A roundabout way of saying: 'Do not be so perpetually satiated with lust as to kill the spirit of our love'.
9. *Intrim*: an allusion to the duration of their separation; fundamentally a reference to their excited spirit-of-love-excluding lustfulness of the present. Hence the appeal with which the poem opens.
10. *contracted new*: recently betrothed. But the more literal meaning of 'recently joined together physically' is the main one here.
11. *banckes*: seashores. *see*: meet.
12. *Returne of love*: turn back again to each other by reason of love. 'Of' was frequently used to mean 'through', 'by reason of'. *blest*: endowed with healing virtues, happy. *view*: refers only ostensibly to reunited lovers, happier because of their mutual vigil across the ocean; primarily refers to how a return of love would affect the appearance of their present physical relationship. There is nothing, however, which suggests that Shakespeare hopes for or expects such a change, as we infer from the last word of the sonnet: he is marking time, commentating, accepting the situation.
13. *As*: This is always emended to 'Else' or 'Or', but I see little justification for either of these changes, although the former is graphically just plausible. Admittedly 'As' is clumsy and difficult, but in the absence of anything convincingly better I retain Q. It is best taken in the sense of '(It is) as (if it were to) call it Winter'. *it*: (i) our separation; (ii) this distressing physical episode between us.
14. *rare*: (i) exceptional; (ii) unexpected and therefore unlikely.

57

A more direct tone of heavily sarcastic bitterness is introduced for the first time into the Q sequence. All the psychological evidence points to the subject of this sonnet being the Friend and not the Mistress; the causes for such bitterness are made obvious enough in sonnets in which there is no doubt of the masculine identity of the person addressed. So far (if we accept the Q sequence), there has been little evidence of such ill-usage of Shakespeare by his Mistress.
1. *tend*: see 53, 2, n.
3-4. Forthright and even savage irony, reflected in the rhythm, rescues

Shakespeare's state of subservience from utter pusillanimity.
5-8. Establish without doubt the bitterly sarcastic tone.
9. *jealious*: *suspicious*. A frequent 16th- and 17th-century spelling, which need not, however, denote pronunciation of three syllables.
10. *your affaires suppose*: 'make any guess as to what you may be doing'.
12. '(I dare think of nothing) except of how happy you make those in whose company you are.'
13-14. 'A man in love is so foolish that he forgives, as I do, even your physical infidelities.' *Will*. A play on (i) Shakespeare's name (see 135, 136 and 143, 13), and a combination of (ii) carnal appetite, lust, and (iii) choice, pleasure, i.e. the choice of your lust.

58

A less emotional version of 57 in which Shakespeare acknowledges to himself, so to speak, his state of dependence, and determines to act the part of an unselfish lover.
1. *That God*: the God of Love.
2. Shakespeare acknowledges the unfaithful nature of his friend, but maintains his own efforts to love him selflessly. This is an important psychological factor in the *Sonnets*: Shakespeare knows his friend for what he is, but wishes to change him by the purity of his own love.
3. 'Demand from you an account of how you have been spending your time.'
5-6. 'Let me endure your absence from me, which is like being in prison for me, for the sake of your liberty (which as your lover, wishing you well, I should desire).'
7. '(Let me) subdue my impatience, experience each insult as a matter for forbearance.' 'Patience' is the object of '(Let me) tame'. Patience is a merely temporary state of mind; sufferance, especially in the Elizabethan connotation of 'allowing things to take their course without opposition' is an altogether loftier and more permanent emotion.
8. *injury*: insult. (Shakespeare wishes to allow himself to be insulted without accusing the insulter.)
9. *charter*: 'privilege', with the added sense of 'immunity'.
10. *priviledge*: license.
11 *To*: according to, to correspond with.
12. Leaves little doubt that the Friend was playing fast and loose in all directions.
13. *I am to waite*: I am obliged to (i) await (ii) serve.
14. pleasure: (i) general desires (ii) carnal pleasure. This line also carries the sense: 'I am in no position to criticize our physical relationship even if it is against my conscience.'

59

The writer in Shakespeare, choosing the somewhat literary theme of Ovid's cyclical creed, ironically and light-heartedly excuses the man for celebrating so unworthy an object as his friend. Lee, in his edition of 1907, aptly quotes these passages from Shakespeare's old favourite, Golding's translation of Ovid's *Metamorphoses*: '... In all the world, but altring takes new shape', and 'Things passe perchaunce from place to place: yit all from whence they came Returning, doo unperrished continew still the same'. The precise metaphysics of this idea are not important in the sonnet, however; the general notion is one of 'what is, has been before', or, in the words of *Ecclesiastes*: 'There is no new thing under the sun'.

1-4. 'If there is nothing new, if all that is has been before, how are we tricked into imagining that what we write is original, when the same thing has in fact been said before?'

3. *invention*: used here in the sense of 'literary composition'. *amisse*: 'mistakenly', perhaps 'calamitously'.

4. *burthen*: a play on (i) load (ii) refrain, i.e. verse in general (iii) birth.

5. *record*: recollection.

7-8. 'Show me some description of you in the time since writing was invented.'

10. 'To the consummate miracle of your body.'

11. *mended*: 'improved', with the possible addition of the sense of 'restored to health'.

12. 'Whether the succeeding cycles of time produce identical people.'

12. *revolution*: alteration.

13. *wits*: possibly this is slightly derogatory and thus self-deprecatory.

14. Can be read as a compliment, by understatement; but is almost certainly meant literally.

60

1. *pibled*: pebbled.

2. *our minuites*: the minutes of our lives, pushing each other forward.

4. *sequent*: following upon one another.

5. *Nativity*: This abstract noun, with astrological connotations, stands for the concrete 'newborn child'. *maine of light*: The sphere of heaven. Again, this image recalls the astrological conception of the position of a birth in the Zodiac. There is an echo of the sea-imagery of 1-4 in 'maine'.

7. Malignant (astrological) influences scheme his downfall, i.e. he is doomed from the start. (See 15, 4-6 and notes).

8. *confound*: 'destroy', with the added sense of 'contradict'.

9. *transfixe*: 'destroy', *florish*: bloom.

10. See 2, 2. *paralels*: (i) wrinkles (ii) trenches in a field.
11. 'Devotes particular attention to destroying the most beautiful things.' It becomes increasingly evident that 'Time' in these sonnets is a way of living as well as the mere succession of days which the word ordinarily denotes. 'Time', people's 'sequent toile' towards material progress, as well as the conventional view of time which arises from this, is seen as something actively opposed and in strong contrast to 'natures truth'.
13. *times in hope*: not just 'future times' (because if Shakespeare meant this, then nothing, not even his own verse, stands 'but for his sieth to mow') but 'times when things will be looked upon differently (i.e. when "natures truth" prevails), and which exist only in my imagination (hope)'. Also: for (my verse shall be valid to) those whose own sense of time is correct, and not in opposition to "natures truth."

61

4. *shadowes*: See 27, 10, n.
7. 'To discover my faults and how I waste my time.'
8. *skope*: object, aim. *tenure*: a legal term: a transcript of a document containing only the substance of the original. The phrase 'the skope and tenure of thy Jelousie' means 'the object and essential part of your suspiciousness'. The point of the sonnet is that any moral concern for Shakespeare's inner welfare, or any concern about his constancy, is quite beyond the Friend's capacities. The concerns of this haunting image of the Friend conjured up by Shakespeare are projections of his own feelings,
12. In other words: 'since you are incapable of my finer feelings, I have to have them for you'.
13. *wake*: (i) keep awake (ii) stay up late for revelry.
14. There is a suggestion here, as elsewhere, that the Friend kept the sort of company that would seem frivolous to a serious poet. Along with his love, Shakespeare often reveals the solicitude of an older and wiser man for a younger one's welfare.

62

1-4. It is not the self-love itself which obsesses him, but the sin, and the guilty need for it; the poem attempts to deal with this problem, but peters out into the conceit of the identity of his 'self' with the Friend. See 22 and 36.
5. *gratious*: wonderful, lovely.
6. *true*: well-proportioned.
7-8. 'And for the sake of myself I assess notions of merit, and find this self worthier than all others.'

10. *beated*: an agricultural term, still used in Devon, for the practice of slicing off rough turf from moorland in order to turn it into manure. *chopt*: seamed (with 'parallels').
12. 'It would be an iniquity to love my own self as revealed in the mirror.'
13-14. 'It is you, my beloved, who are myself, whom I am praising when I praise myself; I imagine myself beautiful by investing myself with your beauty.' There is an uneasy and tentative identification of the image of the Friend, carried by Shakespeare as his 'self', with the neurotically conceived 'sinne' for which 'there is no remedie'.

63

1-8. *Against*: the subject of this sentence (1-8) is lacking; owing to the extreme length of the predicate 'against' has to be repeated as 'for' at the beginning of the new sentence (1. 9).
2. *chrusht and ore-worne*: crumpled and worn-out.
5. *steepie*: difficult to ascend.
11-12. 'That ("Ages knife" – like Time's scythe) shall never be able to cut down his beauty, though it destroy him.'
13-14. It is the Friend's beauty, his one positive asset, that here obsesses Shakespeare to the exclusion of everything else.

64

1. *fell*: cruel.
2. As Ransom remarks (*The World's Body,* 1938), this line 'bristles with logical difficulties' and 'strongly resists paraphrase'; Shakespeare seems to have anticipated the results of the defacement by Time of the 'rich proud cost' in the adjectives describing 'age'. *cost*: splendour.
4. *brasse*: here symbolizes imperishableness. Perhaps there is also an allusion to the commemorative brass tablets on tombs: thus, ironically, is brass, symbol of imperishableness, used. *mortall rage*: furiousness subject to death. Again, time is identified with an attitude towards it. (See 60,11, n.)
5-8. Lee (ed. 1907) quotes from Golding's Ovid: 'Even so have places oftentymes exchaunged theyr estate. For I have seene it sea which was substanciall ground alate, Ageine where sea was, I have seene the same become dry lond'. Shakespeare could have observed the former on the East Anglian coast, or at certain places in the south-west, and the latter in the south-east.
8. The sea's inroads in one place compensate for the land's egresses in another, and vice versa.
9. *state*: estate: condition.
10. *state*: majesty.

13-14. A more general reason for the sadness of love is given here: because the beloved must go the way of all flesh.

65

1. *Since brasse*... 'there is neither' is elided.
2. *mortallity*: used with the sense of 'deadliness' as well as of 'death'.
3. *this rage*: mortality's.
4. *Whose*: beauty's. *action*: power to preserve itself.
6. *Wrackfull*: destructive.
9. 'How shall the beloved (here identified with beauty, 'times best Jewell') escape being encased in a coffin?'
13. *unlesse this miracle have might*: Shakespeare means 'unless I can live poetically and truthfully up to the occasion'. The theme of the preservation of his love through his verse is not a mere vulgar evocation of posterity, but a vindication of the truthfulness of poetry against all odds, including Time and those who, by striving only for their pleasure and material gain, are its slaves.

66

2. *desert*: worth, merit. *borne*: born. The tone of the whole sonnet is extremely pessimistic.
4. *unhappily*: wrongly, capriciously, and in miserable circumstances. Those who are most honoured, i.e. those who are in charge of affairs, are unworthy.
8. *disabled*: pronounced with four syllables: *disabeled*.
9. This line has been connected with the persecution of the theatre in specific years; but 'arte' means 'literature', and Shakespeare was thinking less of the censorship in particular than of the more universal obligation of writers to omit to deal with such subjects as might offend the authorities.
10. *Doctor-like*: with the knowing air of a doctor: i.e. most 'experts' are quacks.
11. *Simplicitie*: the bucolic naïvety of the ignorant countryman.
12. 'Goodness used by evil to advance itself.'

67

This sonnet is usually read as straightforward praise of the Friend at the expense of Shakespeare's environment. The puzzled rather than directly rhetorical tone and form of the questions it poses suggest it as something far from this, however. The badness of the times is not merely an academic point in Shakespeare's theme of the youth's extreme beauty: it signifies his currently gloomy view – a pessimism generated, after all, by the brutal disappointment of his hopes in the young man. The fact is that Shakespeare's love-relationship offered none of those consolations usual to lovers in their prime, and the lifelong concern of poets, for the evils so superbly enumerated in 66. If Shakespeare had been confident in the Friend, then the tone of 67 would have been one of triumph instead it is bitter and perplexed. He seems to say here: 'Nature is not what it was. This beautiful youth *does* live with corruption and *is* corrupt. The explanation of his poetically disturbing lack of that moral beauty which ought to go with his rare physical beauty, is that he happens to be the prototype for a worn-out Nature: she uses and draws upon his real beauty to pretend that she still lives as once she lived'. But at a profounder level – reflected in his use of the words 'infection', 'impietie', 'sinne', 'banckrout' – Shakespeare searches his heart for the reason why Nature is not now what it used to be. The true lover feels himself to be elevated above that worldly and material scheme of things of which he is a part because the altruism of his love imparts to his motives a greater purity than that of 'the world'; Shakespeare can no longer feel this. His unnatural relationship with the Friend has shattered his poetic confidence in Nature itself.

4. *lace*: adorn.

5-6. Superficially, these lines merely elevate the Friend's beauty over everyone's by rhetorically ascribing their use of cosmetics to a universal desire to emulate it; essentially, they question the motives of those who consistently flatter him. 'To paint' frequently meant 'to flatter with specious words'. The 'Rival Poet' has been suggested here, but Shakespeare is alluding to the self-torturing conceits of his own poetic tributes.

7-8. The same question re-phrased. One of the tragedies of homosexual love is its ultimate recourse to artificiality. *poore*: ill-used, abused. *indirectly*: evasively. *Roses of shaddow*: artificial roses.

9-12. 'Why should Nature, who depends for her credit solely upon the effect created by his beauty, though she boasts of so many beautiful people, be allowed to continue to use him as her prototype, since she no longer has anything natural left – not even blood to make real roses in people's cheeks?' *banckrout*: bankrupt.

10. The reference is again to cosmetics, as throughout the following sonnet. Does Shakespeare think of the new, false Nature as a hideously made-up male prostitute, a travesty of his friend and yet a vision of what he might become? *Beggerd of.* destitute of.

12. *gaines?* Most editors move Q's question-mark back to the end of 1. 10, but my paraphrase should make it clear why I do not accept this emendation.

13-14. Essentially these lines mean that Shakespeare is still able to retain the memory of his friend's beauty as it was before its potentialities of worth had been ruined by unnatural lust. In general terms the shift described in this sonnet is from what some writers wrongly call Renaissance 'homosexuality' – which was in fact 'the art of friendship' and all that this, specifically (and I would say by definition) implied outside homosexuality – to a physical relationship.

68

The 'metaphysical' unease of the preceding is replaced in this slighter and less ambiguous sonnet by a confidence in the conceit and a passing attack on the artificialities of the time, especially, it seems, on the practice of wearing wigs made from the hair of the dead.

1. *Thus*: refers to 67. *map*: prototype.

3. *faire*: see 16, 11, n. *borne*: (i) came into fashion; (ii) endured.

10. *it selfe*: refers to the quality of 'those holy antique howers'.

69

A warning to the young man that he is squandering his special beauty.

1-2. 'Viewed externally, you appear to be the perfect object of love'. *parts*: attributes. *mend*: improve upon.

4. Even their true praise resembles the grudging due given a man by his foes.

6-8. In other words, the Friend liberates their envious and 'common' speculations by irresponsibly exposing himself to them, allowing them to 'see' farther. The extended metaphor of the tongue, first the voice of true nature (soule), and then becoming a seeing, guessing and finally smelling organ is clumsy but peculiarly apposite, and has fairly obvious connotations.

10. The suggestion is that the young man's deeds are causing Shakespeare misgivings: he grows 'common' (l. 14) because of them.

11. *churls*: 'they' who 'look into', etc.

13-14. Shakespeare here seems to admit that his friend's behaviour has 'the rancke smell of weeds', though he dismisses the 'world's' reason for thus condemning it, and substitutes one of his own, which is that he is in danger of becoming part of the 'bad' scheme of things condemned in 67. Thus the pun on 'soyle': (i) blemish; (ii) ground, suggests the metaphor of the young man choked by weeds, in the 'common' soil. *soyle*: The New Oxford Dictionary can cite only this line for the suggested meaning of 'solution', and it seems unlikely. The stinking weeds *motif is* developed in 94.

70

That 'nearly all commentators', as Rollins correctly states (*New Variorum* I, 183), 'recognize the inconsistency of the picture of the friend as given in 70 with that painted in other sonnets' seems to be due to a combination of misreading, over-literalness of approach and failure to appreciate the frequent shifts of tone and mood in what was, after all, almost certainly a private series of love-poems. This sonnet is primarily consolatory and deals with the question of ill-repute, which, as Shakespeare logically points out in the opening line, is not in itself a 'defect'. If it is read carefully enough it will readily be seen that nowhere does he state that there is *now* no actual defect; in l. 11 he hints that there is. He has been at pains to make this distinction in the closing lines of 69. As to the problems of inconsistency presented by 'pure unstayined prime' and 'past by the ambush of young daies': Shakespeare has been alluding in the preceding sonnets to the dangers of the young man's *present* conduct, for which he has not yet by any means emotionally *condemned* him, and for which he often attempts to excuse him, as here; the latter phrase must not be taken literally, but figuratively – Lee's surmise that some years had passed is nothing short of ridiculous. Shakespeare meant (consolingly, but no doubt with unconscious irony) that the youth had managed to resist some temptations. Many of these sonnets must be read as examples of poetic truthfulness and wisdom expressing itself in a sharp involuntary complexity of language which cuts across, and conflicts with, a much coarser emotionalism. Sometimes the poetic sharpness is much in evidence, and has a cutting edge of irony or *double entendre,* as in 67; in others, as here, it emerges in the more strictly technical complexities of 'metaphysical' exposition.

2. *marke*: target.

3. 'Suspicion (of vice) goes hand-in-hand with beauty'.

5-8. The general sense seems to be: 'so long as you are good, slanders about you merely prove your greater worth, since slander goes with beauty, and you will have resisted all the temptations of a severely testing period of your life'. It is a somewhat pointless argument, and those puzzled by the supposed inconsistency of the picture of the young man in this sonnet should note the conditional clause.

11-12. 'It will not suffice to rely on your former reputation in order to silence current slanders upon your name, for these are due to envy, and this is always rampant.' *inlarged*: set free.

13-14. A curiously weak and obscure ending. It seems to mean: 'If your true beauty were not concealed by the usual ill-repute which goes with beauty, then you alone would be king of all hearts.' *owe*: possess.

71

This poem was written in a mood of such deep depression that it achieves an effect of quite gay sarcasm. 'Vile' is used ironically, and with due recognition, as Theodore Spencer observed, of its 'conventionality and flatness'. The other conventional adjectives –'sweet', 'wise' – are used with almost equal irony.

2. *Then*: an old form of 'than'.

4. *vildest*: 'vilde' was a common spelling of 'vile'.

10. *compounded*: blended.

12-14. The suggestion is that the youth's love is so absurdly slight that any post-mortem on it would be received with mockery.

72

A 'serious' and non-ironic development of the theme contained in the last three lines of 71; Shakespeare now directs his venom at himself.
4. *prove*: discover.
9-10. 'In case you feel impelled by loyalty, for the sake of your love for me, to impart to me virtues which I do not possess.'
11 *be*: let it (my name) be...
13-14. These lines imply that Shakespeare was as deeply depressed by his inability to make poetic sense of his predicament as by the predicament itself.

73

4. *bare ruin'd quiers*: a highly compressed metaphor in which Shakespeare visualizes the ruined arches of churches (or perhaps those of the ruined monasteries dating from Henry VIII's reign), the memory of singing voices still echoing in them, and compares this with the nearly naked boughs of early winter with which he identifies himself.
9-12. The image is that of a fire choked by its own ashes.

74

3. *interest*: the only part of his life which has any worth is his poetry; but the line also means that some fame will accrue to him through his poetry.
11-12. A reference to the baseness of the body in comparison with the spirit, owned by the young man (l. 8), and the creator of the poetry; very likely Shakespeare was thinking of Marlowe's death.
13-14. Once again Shakespeare attempts to dispel his depression by identifying his love for the Friend, and the Friend himself, with his immortal part. Shakespeare believed in the immortality of poetry on the grounds of its enduring truthfulness rather than the fact that it would be 'on lips of living men'.

75

3. *for the peace of you*: Possibly this may carry the meaning of 'to enjoy you in peace', but primarily it means 'to establish peace and order in yourself'. The allusion is of course to the young man's demeanour and its effect on Shakespeare.
5-8. 'Now proud to be intimately associated with you, then fearful that your easy success in society will steal you from me; now considering it better to be alone with you, then falling to the temptation of showing myself off with you in public.' Line 6 clearly refers to Shakespeare's fears for his friend's integrity.
11-12. 'Having or wanting nothing except that which comes from you or must

come from you in the course of things.' The 'delight' which 'must from you be tooke' is faintly ironic.
14. 'Either I eat everything on my table, or I have nothing – nothing being on it'.

76

This sonnet is in defence of Shakespeare's highly personal style rather than in the self-derogatory mood of 72; and it still stands as a notable apology for direct personal poetry as against verse written in fashionable vein on 'impersonal' themes.
3. *with the time*: in the fashion.
4. *compounds strange*: compositions original in form; but also, perhaps, an allusion to the craze for compound words amongst some contemporaries. The reference is singularly apposite to Chapman.
5-6. There may be a reference here to the dying out of the vogue for the sonnet-form (c.1600), and Shakespeare's continued use of it. Certainly he seems to be arguing for simplicity in verse-forms; these became much more complex towards the turn of the century.
8. *their*: every word's. *where*: from whence.
11-12. Not self-derogatory: love is the only worthwhile theme, Shakespeare hints, and he is providing a valid 'new' variation on this theme. The figure of the sun in the following lines emphasizes his confidence in the poetic propriety of this: the implication is that the sun is permanent and the mystery of its daily death and renewal is unsolved, so that to turn to 'new found methods' is fruitless. Only love can tell 'what is told'.

77

Probably, as originally suggested by Nicholson in *Notes and Queries* in 1869, written to accompany a gift of a table book with a looking-glass on one cover and a portable sun-dial on the other.
1. *were*: emended by all editors since Gildon (1710) to 'wear': but in view of the 'wrinckles' and 'mouthed graves' of lines 5 and 6, Q seems to fit into the mood of the sonnet quite as well, if not better. The tone of the whole may be summed up: 'You are growing older now, and growing up, and showing signs of it; things are becoming more serious: the beauty of your extreme youth is no longer enough except as a reminder of the task before you...'
5-6. Not, as some commentators take it, an allusion to the age of the Friend, but a way of saying: 'When you look into the mirror the lines you see on your face will remind you that the grave is waiting for you like an open mouth'.
9. *Looke what*: see 37, 13 and 11, 11, n.
10. *blacks*: universally emended, and not unreasonably, to 'blanks'; but

Nicholson's argument that the 'leaves' were made of slate 'of some black composition' fitted together with a clasp, citing an instance, is at least cogent enough to justify retention of Q.
11-12. 'You shall find those children taken care of, who shall be delivered from your brain, and (by writing them down before you forget them, on the tables conveniently provided with this mirror and dial) your mind will become permanently used to them.' The necessary emergence into awareness of ageing and death, being unwelcome notions to the mind of a young man, is compared by Shakespeare to the birth of children: this awareness will be 'nurst' – cared for – by being preserved in the table-book.
13. *These offices*: the duty of recording your fleeting awarenesses of your own impermanence in this book.

78

1-4. Shakespeare means that his poems written to the Friend have been so inspired that poets, whose modes of expression do not otherwise resemble his own, have followed his example and now also write verse inspired by him. The implication is that Shakespeare's work is superior to theirs, and that they have even gone so far ('got my use') as to crib some of his own habits of diction and style.
5-8. 'The dumbe' who has 'heavie ignorance' is Shakespeare himself; the learned and graceful poet whose verse is now improved, being inspired by the Friend, is the so-called 'Rival Poet'. *learneds*: the learned man's.
9-14. Shakespeare makes it abundantly clear that he regarded true poetry as a personal statement of a personal situation, and not as a matter of 'Art'– i.e. scholarship, learning and philosophy: what to-day we should call 'thought'. Essentially what Shakespeare is saying is that he loves the Friend and that therefore in his view he is writing true poetry about him; the poetry of others, particularly that of the Rival Poet, has its genesis in their admiration of what Shakespeare has written of him, and is therefore based on an idea, it is not inspired.

79

The argument here is that whereas the Rival Poet or poets use the Friend's beauty as their theme, Shakespeare truly loves him.
3. *gracious*: pleasing.
5. *thy lovely argument*: the theme of your beauty.
11. *affoord*: offer.

80

In this sonnet Shakespeare seems to have been depressed by at least the stylistic superiority of the Rival's poems over his own; only the final line carries any of the confidence of the preceding.

11. *wrackt*: wrecked.

13. *If*: The capitalization is probably accidental; it might indicate emphasis.

81

1-2. 'Whether I survive you or vice versa.'

3. *from hence*: from now.

12. *breathers of this world*: present generation.

82

The same theme as 78, with Shakespeare's dislike of rhetoric and stylistic devices rather more emphatically phrased. The argument is that although any poet is entitled to praise or write about the Friend, Shakespeare's poems about him are true, whereas theirs are false, flattering and artificial. The implied criticism of the Friend, in accepting these verses, should not be missed.

2. *attaint*: dishonour, censure.

3. *dedicated words*: 'the verses prefaced by a dedication to you', as well as 'verses written with you in mind.'

4. *blessing every booke*: by 'overlooking' them the Friend 'blesses' them.

5. 'You are as clever and wise as you are beautiful.'

6-8. Presumably Shakespeare's 'rival' had appealed to the Friend's learning; Shakespeare here admits that he has not the capacity to do this, but in the lines following he hints at a connection between 'learned' poetry and artificiality.

11. *simpathizde*: truthfully (and sympathetically, because you are beautiful) described.

12. *thy true telling friend*: Shakespeare himself.

13-14. i.e. they take someone already naturally beautiful and abuse their descriptive powers describing him, since their real talent is the artificial one of *constructing* beautiful things or people.

83

The tone here is faintly ironic and differs from the other 'Rival' sonnets in its quiet assurance that, about poetry and its proper themes at least, Shakespeare knows best. Clearly the Friend was not only a prey to flattery, but also felt that Shakespeare himself had not been flattering enough to him. The whole is a subtle rebuke, though perhaps deliberately above the Friend's head.

1. *painting*: here continues the meanings of 'representing in words' and 'beautifying': the sense of the line is that the Friend's beauty is enough in itself.

2. *faire*: See 16, 11, n.
4. Surely a reference to the fulsome dedications of the time; it also suggests that Shakespeare had received money from the Friend.
6-7. Again, these lines are written less in praise of the Friend than as a sarcastic indication of Shakespeare's view of his contemporaries' dedicatory verses.
9. *This silence.* Probably refers not to literal silence, but to the absence of fashionable eulogy in Shakespeare's poems to the Friend. (It would not have taken a man of any great sensibility to discern a certain note of criticism in some of sonnets 20-82.)
11-12. The sense is, broadly, that Shakespeare celebrates the Friend as he is, whereas other poets artificialize him with false praise and thus render him – in their verses – a lifeless creature.
14. *both your Poets*: clearly refers to Shakespeare and his rival, and implies at least some genuine respect for the latter (even if not for the other eulogists of the Friend).

84

A reiteration of the theme of the preceding sonnet.
1-2 'The person who says most about you (i.e. Shakespeare) can say no more than that you are yourself alone.' (The 'which' in l. 1 is relative.) The wry and subtle implication is that only he who says 'the most' about the Friend, without the eulogy and artificiality alluded to in 82, 83 and here, is entitled to draw the conclusion expressed in the final couplet: that the Friend's beauty has, after all, a curse attached to it. The 'rivals' do not go deep enough to see that.
2. *alone,*: the comma, otherwise unnecessary, points the meaning: you are only your beautiful self when alone – then you cannot be tainted with the 'curse' of l. 13.
5-8. The poet who cannot dignify his subject at all is talentless; but whoever writes of you need only write of you as yourself to achieve this.
10. A sidelong allusion to the Friend's faults as well as to his beauty.
11. *counter-part*: copy. *fame*: make famous.
12. Probably refers to the success of the 'Rival Poet'; it is unlikely, in view of what we have read about poetry in the preceding sonnets, that Shakespeare, in his present mood, set much store by mere style.
13-14. a *double-entendre*: (i) 'Your beauty is fatal to your praisers, since being beyond praise, you make theirs look absurd.' (ii) 'The curse in you is that, being beautiful but also doting on praise, you attract the worst kind of flattery, thus debasing yourself.'

85

As I read this sonnet, Shakespeare pays a tribute to the poetic authority of the 'Rival' (without committing himself on the eulogies of his imitators), to the extent that he admits that, in a figurative sense, it silences himself. This is an oblique way of acknowledging the blow which the Rival's work has struck at Shakespeare's poetic confidence. But, while granting the Rival an authentic poetic skill superior to his own, Shakespeare implies that his interest in the Friend, though obviously inspired, is academic in comparison with his own passionate involvement.

1. *in manners*: in decency.
3. 'Preserve their fineness by their superb and fashionable style'. 'Reserve' is used in the semi-legal sense of ensuring that a property is kept in the same hands. Shakespeare's muse is 'tounge-tide', not in a literal sense, but in contrast to this emphasis on merely stylistic excellence. (Possibly 'their' should be 'thy', as in 26, 12, etc; but this makes little difference to the sense.)
4. *fil'd*: polished.
7. *Himne*: Almost certainly an allusion to Chapman as the 'Rival'. (See Introduction.)

86

The magnificence of this sonnet depends not upon what is frequently taken as ironic praise, but upon the force and sincerity of Shakespeare's admiration for the Rival. The fact that the Rival *was* able to 'fill his line' with the 'countinance' of the Friend, and thus reduce Shakespeare to envy and despair, makes the unequivocal nature of Shakespeare's admiration clear.

1. *proud full saile*: verse like that of a ship going full sail with the wind. Undoubtedly a compliment to the technical accomplishment of the Rival.
2. *(all to precious)*: the brackets merely serve instead of two hyphens: 'all-too-precious'.
3. *inhearce*: imprison, as in a tomb.

5-6. It is difficult to reconcile that view of the sonnet which states that it is almost wholly ironic praise with these lines. Despite the implied criticism that the Rival's *métier is* over-metaphysical, the tribute 'above a mortall pitch' rings true. The phrase 'by spirits taught to write', together with lines 1-10, suggests Chapman as the Rival more strongly than any other of the many unknown factors involving these sonnets (see Introduction).

7-8. Shakespeare, in absolving the Rival's 'compiers by night' of responsibility for his poetic paralysis, implies some familiarity with and respect for them. *astonished*: amazed, paralysed with fear.

9. Almost certainly a reference to Chapman and his claim to have been inspired

by Homer.
10. Usually taken to mean that the spirit 'gulled', that is 'fooled', the Rival with what it told him; the line, however, is not a criticism, but a poetic tribute of great depth. 'Gull' here is used more in the sense of 'to trick' than 'to fool': Shakespeare means that all poetic knowledge, 'intelligence', is a curse to a poet in his ordinary, day-to-day material life. In listening to it 'by night', inside himself, when the material world is 'asleep', he is being 'gulled' into an attempt to achieve truth-inspired behaviour, and will indeed appear a 'gull', a fool or a dupe, in the eyes of the world. Far from being critical, these lines represent one of the most inspired, subtle and profound tributes from one poet to another in all literature.
13. This line does not mean 'when you approved his verse', but 'when I saw that he had successfully created an image of you'. This does not imply that the Rival had written of the Friend in the same kind of personal terms as Shakespeare in these sonnets, but merely indicates Shakespeare's recognition of the poetic authenticity of the Friend as the Rival's vehicle of inspiration. *fild*: filled.
14. This admittedly difficult line means: 'When I saw that the Rival was writing of you with poetic authenticity, I felt robbed of my own inspiration'.

87

1 *deare*: precious; but also 'grievous'.
2. *estimate*: value, 'worth to me'.
3. The superficial sense of 'your great beauty and worth endow you with the privilege of contracting out of your relationship with one so less worthy' is given greater ironic force by the more personal sense, 'my love for you knows no bounds, of which you are fully aware' (see l. 2).
4. *determinate*: out of date: a term used in legal conveyances.
8. *pattent*: right to your love. *swerving*: returning to you (see l. 3).
9-12. The sense is: 'You gave yourself to me when you were either ignorant of what your beauty could command, or mistaken in the type of person I was.' (The primary difference is that Shakespeare is not worthy; a less obvious one is that Shakespeare's loving concern with the Friend's character might well seem to him homiletic and irritating.)
14. This may refer to the Friend as well as to Shakespeare himself. *no such matter*: no such thing.

88

This sonnet clearly reflects the psychologically peculiar nature of Shakespeare's devotion to the Friend. It has a force far beyond that of a mere 'metaphysical' conceit, and suggests something of the purity of spirit from which Shakespeare derived much of his poetic power. He is now, as has been pointed out, considering (with a much greater sense of immediacy) doing what he had said he would do in 49. Unless we understand that Shakespeare meant this literally – and it does appear, superficially, after all, preposterous – we have little chance of understanding the *Sonnets* as a whole.

1. *set me light*: despise me.

2. 'And regard even my true merits with contempt.'

3-4. It is important to realize that Shakespeare meant this literally, and was not saying it to bolster up a conceit. The psychological intention is twofold: not only does Shakespeare intend to love to the bitter end, but also he proposes to demolish the edifice of his own ego by this process of identification with the Friend. Unrequited love becomes an instrument of severe self-criticism, even of self-destruction.

6-7. 'I can support your case against me by revealing many hitherto concealed faults with which I am infected'.

89

1-2. 'If you claim that you forsook me for an offence or a fault, then I will agree with you, even though your claim be false'.

3. 'If you say I am lame, I will pretend to be so (in order to protect the integrity of your word).'

6. 'To make your inconstancy look excusable.' Shakespeare has no illusions about the treacherous nature of the Friend: he does not call him worthless directly, only because he loves him; and because the lesson Shakespeare is determined to learn from all this is that, however worthless the Friend is, Shakespeare is more worthless.

8. 'I will end our familiarity, and pretend not to know you when we meet.'

90

Shakespeare here alludes to a misfortune, or a series of misfortunes, which had overtaken him in his professional or domestic life, or both, and which has no direct bearing upon his relationship with the Friend.

4. 'And do not come in casually to witness some future grief.'

91

3. *though new fangled ill*: 'new-fangle' is a verb meaning 'to make with an eye to fashion and newness'; obviously Shakespeare regarded the extravagant late Elizabethan fashions, particularly in male clothing, as hideous.

5. *humor*: disposition, temperament.

7. 'But this delight in a favourite pleasure is not my way of attaining happiness'

8. *better*: surpass.
9-12. Means that the Friend is in himself superior to all the delights enumerated above; the probable implication is that he contains within himself or possesses all the qualities or skills involved in those delights.
13-14. While Shakespeare has the Friend's love he is happier than all others – but if it is taken away then he has nothing at all.

92

1. It is increasingly evident that while the Friend had tired of Shakespeare, he was seeking some face-saving means of ending the relationship. *But*: obviously a link with the preceding sonnet.
2. *tearme of life*: 'for as long as I live'; the phrase has a legal connotation, and the sonnet itself is partly an ironic piece of advice to the Friend on how to get out of something which is legally binding for life.
5-6. 'I need not fear the worst wrong of all – when you finally reject me – for with this will come death.'
8. *humor*: fancy.
10. 'My life ceases when your love for me ceases.'
11-12. Shakespeare finds consolation in the fact that if he loses the Friend's love then he will 'die'; the 'death' referred to here is a state of mind in which nothing will matter. It is evident that Shakespeare is already dangerously near desiring such a state.
13-14. A further reason for self-torment: perhaps the Friend has already rejected him, but he does not know it. There is a strong sense, in this part of the sequence, of being *kept alive,* painfully, by the sheer beauty of the Friend (see 93).

93

1. The inescapable inference is that Shakespeare will 'hang on', deliberately allowing himself to be deceived.
2. *loves face*: both 'the aspect of love' and 'love as expressed in your face'.
3. *alter'd new*: changed.
7. *manies*: E. E. Cummings's 'mostpeople' is probably the nearest modern equivalent to this possessive plural noun.
13-14. The Friend's beauty, and his control over himself as possessor of that beauty, are here seen as separate: his beauty will become an inspiration of the devil if he does not match it spiritually.

94

The psychological situation behind this part of the sequence (from 88) is more clearly revealed in this sonnet. The Friend as he is at present can be clearly visualized: out of love with Shakespeare, but nevertheless somewhat coldly disclaiming Shakespeare's probably passionate accusations as hysterical; possibly refusing to acknowledge the end of his love for Shakespeare when begged to do so, because this would involve a tacit admission of the nature of his present activities. It is fairly evident that the Friend, among his other faults, was a hypocrite and a face-saver. It is likely that although he had ceased to care for Shakespeare, his vanity desired, and perhaps needed, to retain Shakespeare's idealistic admiration. As Empson has stated in his famous discussion of this sonnet, it 'is a piece of grave irony'; but the irony is intermittent and complicated, being expressed in the tone rather than in what is said. Shakespeare means what he says in lines 1-8; the irony lies in the fact that he knows perfectly well that the Friend is not that kind of person at all, but only seems to be – and in the desperate rarity of such detached people. This is what the Friend – because of his beauty, and because of the potentiality for good which Shakespeare undoubtedly originally divined in his character – ought to be like. What he *is* like is a festering lily: as Empson says: '... even the best people must be continually on their guard, because they become the worst... once they fall from their perfection'. The remarkable thing about this assessment of the Friend's worth is that Shakespeare has not decided to try to cure himself of his love for him; he has to tell the truth, but still believes in the fact of his beauty and in its healing power, as may be deduced from many of the sonnets that follow.

1. i.e. the Friend, who could 'kill' Shakespeare by leaving him, but will not do so. It is important to understand that in lines 1-8 of this sonnet Shakespeare is contrasting the abstract notion of a saintly character, who has power to hurt but does not exercise it, with his concrete experience of the Friend, who does exactly the same, but whose motives are far from saintly. Beyond his ironic acceptance of the Friend's treacherousness in this sonnet, Shakespeare, by this contrapuntal device of laying the concrete against the abstract, is questioning the validity of superficial virtue in man. He dealt with this problem at length in the character of Angelo.

6. *from expence*: literally, 'from what they give away, or lose.'

8. The others, having no control, are not true owners of their beauty, but merely *spenders* of it: the word 'steward' implies the notion, strong in the *Sonnets,* that beauty and virtue need to be controlled, and that those favoured with them can, and should, aspire to more than mere stewardship of them. But the loophole, through which Shakespeare has consistently found hope, is, at this point in the sonnets, left intact: 'excellence' must survive, it cannot be destroyed. It is in the following six lines that Shakespeare first shows signs of absolute despair. Until now he could always believe, to some extent, in the Friend's outward embodiment of beauty and virtue; now, his internal rottenness leaves Shakespeare no alternative but to deliver the warning of the last line.

14. This line occurs in the play *The Reign of King Edward III* (1596), parts of which have been attributed to Shakespeare by some scholars, with Chambers's approval, if not total agreement.

95

Contains a similar warning to the preceding so far as the Friend is concerned, but goes forward poetically, so far as Shakespeare is concerned, by considering the paradox of beauty and evil. His poetic absorption in this problem must have represented some psychological relief to Shakespeare.
6. *sport*: sexual promiscuity.
7-8. This is ironic: 'because you are so beautiful, you get off lightly.'
11-12. 'Beauties vaile' is the subject: The essential sense is: 'Your outward appearance causes even your worst actions to seem fair, so irreconcilable are they with its extreme beauty'.

96

1-4. 'Some excuse you and some criticize you, but it is indisputable that faults, in you, appear graces.'
9-12. A fairly straightforward comparison of the Friend to a merciless wolf, with his admirers as his lamb-like victims.
13-14. A repetition of the conclusion of 36. Thus has been held to be a printer's error, but it is more likely that Shakespeare intended it, in a double sense, as an ironic echo from a time when he had not been fully aware of the Friend's character.

97

This seems to begin a new short series, whose tone is quite different from that of the preceding. It is unlikely that the 'absence' referred to is anything other than literal. Compared with some of the sonnets that have come before, the tone here appears academic. Shakespeare does not seem to be so wholly engaged with his subject-matter. Brooke's comment, in his 1936 edition, that 97-99 'are written as if the poet's heart was not much in them' seems justified. It is possible that they became misplaced in the sequence, and that they really belong somewhere between 20 and 30; but it is just as easy to believe that Shakespeare wrote them, perhaps on his return from a stay in the country, or away from London and the Friend, in an 'academic' rather than an intense state of mind.
2. *?*: This and the two following question-marks are purely exclamatory in function.
10. *But hope of Orphans*: to have no more hope than an orphan.
13. *dull a cheere*: such low spirits.

98

2. *proud pide*: wonderfully variegated.
4. *heavie* Saturne: Saturn represented Melancholy. *heavie*: sad, mournful.
14. *shaddow*: 'a fanciful representation of you'.

99

A poor sonnet which, however, follows on directly from 98. Other fifteen-line sonnets have been noted, but not on this pattern, which seems accidental or haphazard. Line 5 seems to be the odd one out.
1. *forward*: early.
6. *condemned for*: condemned on account of (stealing your hand's whiteness).
7. *marjerom*: marjoram.

100

Here opens a new and entirely different series of sonnets (100-115), addressed to the young man. From the abrupt change in tone and from internal evidence it is clear that some time had elapsed since the series ending with 96 had been written. The suggestion that Shakespeare had been successfully occupied with writing plays for the public is by no means a stupid one, since most of his life was taken up with thus activity. He seems to have returned to his love of the Friend, but to be addressing him from a greater distance – as if he were now confident of his poetic prowess, and was speaking not as an untried poet, but as a successful one. Time and Change, not the Friend's faults, become the object of his poetic attack; he concentrates on the Friend's virtues (see 112, 5-6, n.), investing Time with his previous apprehension of his evil parts. Time, together with Shakespeare's condemnation of his own recent literary activities, are seen as the enemies of the Friend's beauty and goodness. The result is more elegant and sonorous, but does not, as he explains in 102, express his love with such force. If he had been devoting himself to other interests, then this is easily acceptable. Now he returns, in these sonnets, almost as if ashamed of his pursuit of material gains (see 100, 4), to his original poetic theme. It is not long before it again possesses him to the exclusion of everything else.

But there is a further explanation for the new confidence, the maturity, and the absence of neurotic doubts and fears. There is every reason to assume that Shakespeare had outgrown his physical passion for the Friend (the fact that he had done so would not have deterred him from loving him in that idealistic manner the attainment of which had been the subject of so many of the earlier sonnets). (See 110, 13, n.) On the contrary, it is difficult to see what else Shakespeare meant by his 'return' to the Friend, except to make right what had obviously seemed to him to be poetically wrong. In more general terms, the problem may be posed thus: How far is it possible for a man to love a member of his own sex without negating within himself his spiritually necessary heterosexual nature? Homosexual experience is a terrible thing for a predominantly heterosexual person to endure; but because Shakespeare had endured it, and felt himself to be guilty – as a poet – of a crime against nature, he was not going to give up. He had to pursue what was natural in the relationship, to rescue the good from the bad.

3. *furie*: enthusiastic energy.

9. *resty*: sluggish, indolent.

11. 'If there are any wrinkles, then write satires on Time'.

13-14. Essentially an invocation to his Muse – the better part of himself – to rescue the Friend from the wastes of Time (materialism) before it is too late (see 101, 3). As has been mentioned above, Shakespeare very clearly invests Time with all the evil propensities he knows to be in the Friend.

101

4. *dignifi'd*: (thou art) dignified.

6. Truth needs no colours, for it is not artificial.

7. *lay*: put on paper or canvas.

9-14. Shakespeare does not merely mean that his Muse is required to immortalize the Friend's beauty in verse; as he emphasizes in lines 3-4, he regards his poetic duty as something more than a material one. The implication is that 'ages yet to be' will not praise the Friend if he lays himself open to the wastes of Time. The wrinkles on his brow are more than literal.

102

3. *marchandiz'd*: cheapened. *esteeming*: value.

7-8. The nightingale in England stops singing at about the end of July.

8. *his*: it is the cock nightingale that sings, but even if Shakespeare knew this, he is inconsistent in referring to it as 'her' in lines 10 and 13.

11. An ironic allusion to the number of people who are engaged in singing the praises of the Friend – at the wrong end of summer.

103

Here Shakespeare doubts the power of his love to influence the Friend; he sees himself as unable to match the Friend's beauty in his poetry.

1. *poverty*: poor stuff.

7. over-goes: outstrips. *blunt*: clumsy.

104

9. *Dyall hand*: the hand of a clock or watch.
10. *figure*: (i) the number on the face of the clock; (ii) the youthful appearance of the Friend.
13. *age unbred*: ages yet to come.
14. *you*: refers to 'age unbred': 'any of you'.

105

Shakespeare here emphasizes his determination to concentrate on the positive side of the Friend. He has invoked his Muse in 100 to satirize Time, and the inference is that he deliberately wished to avoid satirizing the Friend himself (as, to some extent, he had), but rather to attack the forces which might destroy him. It could be said that this, and some of the other sonnets in this series, are misplaced, but they possess a sonorousness and maturity which makes my explanation, in terms of Shakespeare's changed attitude, more likely. There is an almost doxological deliberateness about this particular sonnet which suggests that what Shakespeare really meant was: 'I realize that, because of what is bad in your character, some people might call you a false God. But my love owes to you a deliberate celebration of those qualities of kindness, beauty and truth which you do in reality possess. My love's duty is to concentrate upon these qualities even in the teeth of the evidence.'

This interpretation is in no sense intended as a paraphrase; but it does account for the peculiarly dogmatic and liturgical quality of the sonnet.

106

2. *wights*: men or women.
3. The beautiful subjects of poems of old made them beautiful.
8. *maister*: possess.
11. *for*: because. *Devining*: guessing.
12. *still*. There is much to be said for 'skill', the emendation generally accepted; but not quite enough to be dogmatic about it. The sense of Q is clear: 'as they (poets of old) could only guess at, not see, your beauty, they *still* could not, etc.' The difficulty of Q lies in the absence of a noun for 'enough' to refer to, and this, not the general sense of the passage, must be the justification for the emendation.

107

There is no doubt that this sonnet contains a specific reference; the difficulty lies in discovering it. Leslie Hotson (*Shakespeare's Sonnets Dated*) develops Butler's earlier suggestion that the defeat of the Armada is the event referred to: the 'mortall Moone', according to Hotson, is the familiar formation of the Spanish fleet. His theory is an attractive and ingenious one, but not wholly convincing. Dr G. B. Harrison claims that the reference is to the genuine anxiety caused by the Queen's entrance, on September 6th, 1595, into her Grand Climacteric (her sixty-third year, representing the association of the mystic numbers seven and nine). He adduces some evidence to show that this event did give rise to much anxiety; but his dating has been seriously challenged, if not effectively shaken, notably by Sir Edmund Chambers. Chambers himself favours 1599, when the Queen was ill; but his reasons are less convincing than those Harrison puts forward for 1595. Another popular but unlikely date is 1603, when Elizabeth died and James VI of Scotland came to the English throne.

There is a theory for almost every year, from 1588 to 1609, but only those mentioned above are worthy of serious consideration. No dating is wholly satisfactory, but Harrison's is by far the most plausible: as he has pointed out, the language of 107 is 'astrological', and the danger to the Queen was 'also astrological'. Much depends on the meaning given to the phrase 'hath her eclipse indur'de' in l. 5: it may mean 'she has suffered eclipse and been annihilated' (as Hotson would have it), or 'she has endured her eclipse and come forth from it triumphantly'. On the whole, the latter interpretation seems the most likely. For further discussion, see Introduction, pp. 10-12.

1-4. Shakespeare associates his fears that he would fall from the Friend's favour (and, possibly, that his own love for him would not endure) with some general recent fears of national disaster which, like his own, have proved unfounded.

6. 'The existence of those who foretold disaster is now a mockery of themselves.'

108

1. *character*: write.

3. *new... now*: unnecessarily emended by most modern editors to 'new... new.'

10. *Waighes not*: attaches no importance to.

109

2. *quallifie*: moderate.

7. *Just*: punctual, exact. *exchang'd*: altered.

8. 'My return to you, with tears, wipes out the offence of my absence.'

10. 'All the faults which assail people of every kind of temperament.'

13-14. 'I hold the Universe worth nothing except that it nurtures you, my Rose.'

110

Many have seen here and in 111 a reference by Shakespeare to his profession as an actor; but as the sonnet has in any case a wider metaphorical application – to his behaviour in general – the point is less material than it has been made to seem.
2. 'Made a fool of myself in public.' The implication, in view of the following lines, is that Shakespeare has prostituted his talents for the sake of public applause. This would not necessarily refer to acting.
3. *Gor'd mine own thoughts*: 'Been untrue to my deepest beliefs.' *sold cheap what is most deare*: means that he has used precious talents for purposes which he regards as unworthy of them.
6. *Asconce and strangely*: indifferently and distantly.
7. *blenches*: (i) side-glances (from truth); (ii) faults. The whole line means: 'I have learned from my mistakes.'
8. 'And trials of worse friendships have proved that ours is the best for me.'
9. 'Now that my fickleness is at an end, take what can have no end' (our love).
10-11. 'I will never again whet my desire by experimenting with others at the expense of an older love.'
13. *next my heaven the best.* Sharp (ed. 1885) pointed out that this is probably an allusion to Shakespeare's mistress; no other explanation serves so well. The absence of nerve-strain from this series of sonnets addressed to the Friend does most strongly suggest the absence of the physical desire for him that is manifested in some of the earlier sonnets. I take this to be a deliberate avowal by Shakespeare of the purity and propriety of his love for the Friend. 'My heaven' here means simply 'my place and object of bliss', i.e. 'my mistress'. 'Heaven' is similarly used in 129, 14. Tucker's gloss (ed. 1924) 'That heaven of mine which is your breast' does not seem a possible interpretation.

111

Whether or not Shakespeare intended to refer to his dependence on the stage in this sonnet, there is a deep irony here which commentators have missed. Shakespeare means what he says, but there is a tone of courtly elegant irony in his acknowledgement to the Friend of these faults: after all, he has in earlier sonnets upbraided the Friend for precisely the same kind of behaviour. The whole sonnet is a piece of elaborate irony.
1. *wish.* All editors except Lintott (ed. 1711) have followed Gildon's emendation (ed. 1710) to 'with'; but Q means simply: 'It is for my sake that you wish fortune to scold...'; or, more colloquially and perhaps more precisely: 'You are correct when you say that I, or what I have represented, deserve this criticism.'
2. Literally, 'the goddess who is guilty of my harmful deeds'. He presumably means the Goddess of Success, but is she not that which the Friend has pursued?

The 'harmfull deeds' may merely be Shakespeare's ironic way of referring to his success in the theatre. In 110 he has treated ambition in a straightforwardly poetic way, in relation to himself and to the love he bears within himself. Here he seems to be repeating what he has said in the previous sonnet, but investing it with irony in view of the Friend's attitude, and of his record and character.
5. There is nothing to suggest that he accepts this 'brand' from other people, or from the Friend; there is a world of difference between proper self-criticism and the falsely motivated opprobrium of society. (See 112, 3.)
6-7. 'I begin to resemble the people I work among, as the dyer's hand the colour of what he works in. *subdu'd*: subjugated to. If Shakespeare is speaking of society in general (which he certainly is in a metaphorical sense, in any case) and not of the stage only, then these lines have an added irony: the Friend's virtues he has elevated above the vulgar material values of society – but he has never been able to do likewise with the Friend himself.
10. *Eysell*: sour vinegar, taken as a preventative of plague.

112

This is a difficult and perhaps confused sonnet, whose cryptic qualities commentators have attempted to remove by numerous emendations, notably of the phrase 'me thinkes y'are dead' (see 14, below). But to change Q here is to rob the sonnet of all coherent meaning.
1-2. The metaphor is that of the scar branded on the forehead of a felon (as was the custom in Shakespeare's time), being 'filled in', i.e. effaced, by the love of the Friend. *vulgar*: public.
3. *ore greene*: cover over so as to hide – as a gardener re-turfs an unsightly patch of earth, or as old buildings are covered by ivy. *alow*: (i) approve, or possibly merely (ii) admit.
5-6. *and I… tounge*: 'I must learn to accept as true praise or blame only what emanates from you'. In view of what Shakespeare knows the Friend is, it is impossible not to assume that here he was addressing the ideal, potential Friend. It is as if Shakespeare had felt that somehow, by concentrating upon only the Friend's virtues, he could make him become what he desired him to become. (See 100, introductory note.)
7-8. It is impossible to make exact sense out of these lines; as Pooler noted (ed. 1918), 'two sentences are crushed into one'. The difficulty may have arisen because of Shakespeare's poetic scrupulousness about the precise identity of the Friend whom he was addressing: this was not the real person, as he himself was, but the imagined and desired ideal (see 5-6 above) who existed only by virtue of the love which Shakespeare, now confidently, felt for him. Thus, the general meaning seems to be: 'No one except you, in your special capacity as my beloved, can influence my now hardened ("steel'd") mind ("sence", but perhaps there is a

play here on "sexual desire, sensual nature"), either for good or for bad.'
10. *Adders sence*: sense of hearing: 'The wicked are estranged from the womb: they go astray a soon as they be born, speaking lies. Their poison is like the poison of a serpent: they are like the deaf adder that stoppeth her ear; Which will not hearken to the voice of charmers, charming never so wisely.' (Psalm 58, 3-5, A.V.)
12. *dispence*: disregard.
13-14. The sense is: 'The world (which does not understand anything about my love for you, or about my desire for the ideal personage that you could become), imagines you as dead, i.e. ordinary and vulgar as it is itself.' He has already said (l. 5) that the Friend is his 'All the world', and here he clearly shows that he knows he is addressing one (the Friend as he actually is) who, like 'all the world besides me', has no understanding of his poetically inspired 'purpose'.

113

1. In other words, 'what I see is determined by my imagination'.
2. My 'ordinary' eye.
3. *part*: divide. (Shakespeare's eye receives images but does not transmit them to his brain, for it is his brain that determines what he shall see.)
4. *effectually*: in effect; in its operation. *out*: not there, removed.
5. *the heart*: the understanding.
6. *it doth lack*: if 'it' refers to the eye, then Malone's emendation (ed. 1790) to 'latch' (to seize, to catch sight of), which has been universally accepted, is of course called for. But if 'it' refers to the 'heart' (the understanding), then Q makes perfect sense, and furthermore the sonnet is not robbed of an essential part of its meaning. For surely Shakespeare's understanding craved to see things as they really were? There is a tone, here ('incapable of more, repleat with you') of weariness and irritation.
7. *his*: usually taken to refer to the eye, but more probably refers to the heart: 'my understanding', Shakespeare is saying, 'is robbed of the living ("quick") things which belong to it'.
8. *his owne vision*: again, Shakespeare is referring to the dependent state of mind which has robbed his poet's understanding of its birthright.
13-14. The phrase 'maketh mine untrue' is usually emended, following Capell, to 'make mine eye untrue', or to an equivalent bringing in 'eye'. But Shakespeare in this couplet is summing up a difficult thought, in keeping with the first twelve lines, and using 'untrue' as a noun. 'My poetic understanding ("most true minde") is so thoroughly surfeited with you that I cannot tell the ordinary truth.' This need not be taken as a criticism of the Friend, but as a piece of self-criticism, the statement of a problem. Shakespeare was committed to the pursuit of a love for the Friend that would satisfy the almost impossibly high standards which, as a

poet, he set himself; here he sees that this is leading him into a form of lying, and it does not satisfy him.

114

A direct sequel to the preceding. Shakespeare explores his problem further.
1. *Or*: 'or', here and in l. 3, is grammatically superfluous. *crown'd with you*: made a monarch by the thought of loving you.
2. *monarks plague this flattery*: an echo of the meaning of the preceding: he is not casting aspersions upon the Friend or upon his love for him, but upon his imagination 'flattering' every shape into that of the Friend. The Friend is Shakespeare's 'all the world', but this is the other side of the coin.
5. *indigest*: shapeless.
8. See 20, 6, for another instance of this notion.
11. *gust*: relish. An extremely sensual word in the context. *greeing*: agreeing.
13-14. The allusion is to a monarch's 'taster', who partakes of all his master's food to ensure that it is not poisoned. Shakespeare emphasizes the poetic doubts expressed in 113.

115

1-4 See 110, 13, n. Shakespeare reiterates in unequivocal terms his poetically inspired purity of purpose.
5. *milliond*: millionfold.
7. *Tan*: spoil.
10. With modem punctuation, this line would read: 'Might I not then say, "Now I love you best"?'
13-14. The couplet states why Shakespeare should not have glorified the present by saying 'Now I love you best', which he admits he has done in l. 2: his love for the Friend was then immature, and is now still growing.

116

This begins a new group of sonnets (116-126), not altogether coherent as a group, and among the most enigmatic of the whole sequence (see Introduction).
1-2. Obviously suggested by the Marriage Service in the Book of Common Prayer: 'If any of you know cause or just impediment...' This sonnet is not about sexual love, but about 'the marriage of true mindes' between two members of the same sex. However, this sort of love, as Shakespeare knows full well, may not only appear homosexual to others (see 121), but also may have passed through a homosexual phase.
2-3. *love is... findes*: 'The sort of love which dies when the situation changes in

any way is not true love.'
4. 'Or inclines, when one of the pair is unfaithful or turns away, to do the same thing.'
8. Refers to the star, representing true love, whose 'height' – i.e. stellar altitude, for the purposes of navigation – is known, but whose 'worth' – influence, mystery and ultimate meaning – is unknown, unfathomable.
13-14. Shakespeare here testifies to his own constancy; the love he here speaks of is certainly not the kind of love he speaks of in 127-152. In the next sonnet he challenges the constancy of the Friend's love in no uncertain terms. The situation seems to have been that the Friend, no doubt flattered at first by Shakespeare's 'return' to him, was soon puzzled by his obviously changed attitude. No doubt he upbraided Shakespeare for this, without understanding, in some such petulant terms as: 'You no longer love me as you used to, because I am older', and so on. The tone of 117, which may well be read as an answer to some such outburst, has none of the submissive tone of earlier sonnets; on the contrary, it is dignified throughout, and written primarily for the ears, not of a petulant young man, but of Truth itself.

117

The tone here suggests that Shakespeare was writing for the ears of his own poetic conscience – of the truth itself – rather than to convince the Friend of anything. He has seen that there is no practical future in his relationship with his Friend, and the final couplet is better taken as a kind of farewell to him, one who is incapable of being loved in reality, than as a plea of self-justification (see 13, below). This theme is developed in the next nine sonnets. Shakespeare has loved truly; but it is impossible to love what cannot be loved in this way (a way which has been detailed in 116). Shakespeare has recognized, it may be inferred, that the Friend will never become the person that the exercise of Shakespeare's true love needs to cause him to become.
1. *scanted*: grudged.
5. *unknown mindes*: strangers, people of no importance.
6. The sense of this line is complicated. As Shakespeare states in the final couplet, as well as in 118, his reasons for turning away from the Friend were not that he had ceased to love him; one of them, indeed, was to prove the 'virtue' of his friend's love. This can only mean that Shakespeare returned to him hoping that he would share his own poetic idealism, and seek to perfect their relationship by rejecting the sexual element in it. However, he acknowledges in this line that in turning away from the Friend and becoming a 'wandring barke' (though guided by love), he was 'giving to Time' something immortal, something that was against Time, namely, that element in their love which had been pure and natural.
7-8. It is here made clear, if it had not been so before, that Shakespeare had

deliberately broken off his relationship with the young man.
10. 'Add all that you suspect to whatever you can prove against me.'
11. *level*: range; aim. The word as used here combines both meanings.
12. *wakened hate*: The Friend probably resented Shakespeare's new and inexplicable attitude towards him as an intolerable and disturbing exhibition of homiletic enthusiasm by an older man.
13. *appeale*: a carefully chosen word. An appeal was, in Elizabethan and Jacobean law, a plea put before a judge. Shakespeare is not appealing to the Friend.

118

The sense of this difficult and subtle sonnet revolves round the meaning, here, of 'rancke of goodnesse'. Here 'goodnesse' means 'success' or 'happiness', rather as in *Macbeth,* IV, iii 136, 'the chance of goodness'. (Cited by Onions.) The essential point is that Shakespeare does not mean that this 'nere cloying' relationship has been virtuous (he implies the opposite), but that it has been fortunate: he has been happy, until he became 'sicke of wel-fare'. Had the relationship been ideal, there would have been no poetic problem to solve. However, he does not claim to have turned sanctimoniously away, out of virtuousness (he admits that this was before there was 'true needing', and by this admission implies that there *was* 'true needing'), but hints that the very nature of the relationship had this effect upon him. A profound and spiritual love-relationship would not have this effect; one with a physical basis, of course, does. Both the metaphor upon which this sonnet is based, and its imagery, make it clear that Shakespeare is not describing a spiritual but a physical relationship: the first two lines alone describe a gluttonous lust, bored by satiety, inventing refinements for itself. That Shakespeare means by 'ills that were not', simply that there was nothing wrong with the personal side of the relationship, that it could have gone on had he not ended it, is revealed by the final couplet (as well as by the sonnet following): he *has,* after all, learned something. What he has learned is, probably, that the further homosexual episodes which he has hinted at in 117, and in l. 6 of the present sonnet, have not 'cured' him, but have poisoned him – but as the next sonnet shows these 'ills' have sent him back to the Friend with a purified love.
2. *eager compounds*: tart or piquant food-inventions: appetizers.
3-4. 'To forestall as yet undiagnosed diseases, we make ourselves ill with purgatives.'
5. *nere*: never.
6. Means that he consorted with people (presumably for homosexual purposes, in order to make his 'appetite more keen' for the Friend) whom he knew to be inferior. A subtle means of describing the corruption of a relationship that is based too much on physical attraction.

7. *meetnesse*: propriety.
9-12. Shakespeare could only be 'cured' by doing more evil. He means by 'healthfull state' and 'rancke of goodnesse', not that he was virtuously happy and ruined it all, but just that he was happy.
14. *Drugs*: the 'drugs' are the 'eager compounds', the purgatives and the 'bitter sawces': the people he consorted with.

119

1-2. The use of the epithet *Syren is* sometimes taken to suggest that 119 was written to or about Shakespeare's mistress; but if he had been alluding to his experiences with women at this stage in the sonnet, he would have written '*Syrens*'. What he is talking about is lust, and this sonnet is clearly to be read in close conjunction with the last. To have drunk potions of *Syren* tears means to have succumbed to Sirens, as Odysseus did not; and to have succumbed not merely to song, but to evil ('distil'd from Lymbecks foule as hell within') entreaties ('teares'). *Lymbecks*: chemical retorts. The allusion, continuing the thought and imagery of the preceding, is to the distilment of medicines – the 'bitter sawces' of 118. The description 'foule as hell within' suggests that these entreaties were unnatural and horrible to Shakespeare.
3. *Applying... to*: as nearly always in Shakespeare, this refers to the medical application of remedies, thus reinforcing the medical imagery of 'distil'd from Lymbecks'.
7. *fitted*: forced out of their usual position by feverish paroxysms: the reference is to protruding eyeballs.
8. *madding*: maddening. 'This madding fever' is lust.
9-12. 'Oh, how I have benefited from my purely lustful exploits! For now I have discovered that a love which was more than merely lustful, though it had its lustful element, has been purified. A love relationship that has been ended, and then re-created in this way, is worth far more than it was at first.'
13. *content*: wish, fulfilment of desire. In view of the 'wel-fare' of which Shakespeare was sick in 118, this probably means 'what I most truly desire'.

120

Here Shakespeare has an attack of remorse for the sense of bewilderment and injury which the Friend must feel, and harks back to his own unhappiness as he expressed it in 34-35. All he is saying here, in the nicest possible way, is that the Friend has no cause to upbraid him for injuries done, since he himself has once grievously wronged Shakespeare. The phrase 'be-friends mee now' implies 'makes it easier for me in a difficult situation'.
2-3. 'I am obliged to feel for you now, and to have remorse for what I have done

to you, in view of how wounded I was when you wronged me.'
4. Shakespeare is here apologizing with his feelings; he never suggests that what he has done was not what he had to do; hence this line, meaning: 'unless I were really a hard man'.
6. *y'have past a hell of Time*: 'you have truly suffered.' It is notable that the tone here is gentle, mature and totally without protest – in great contrast to those earlier sonnets in which he upbraids both the Friend and himself.
8. *crime*: of seducing me.
9. *night... wo*: a direct reference to the action of the Friend which produced sonnets 34-35. *remembred*: reminded.
11-12. Shakespeare's difficulty is that whereas the Friend could (and presumably did) apologize for his 'sensual fault', his 'transgression' is an injury of exactly the opposite nature, and the reasons for it are beyond the Friend's understanding. Hence 13-14.
13-14. '(Except I cannot tender the balm you tendered me) because what you did to me is reason enough for your excusing my offence against you now.'

121

'A difficult and crucial sonnet,' as G. Wilson Knight writes at the beginning of his interesting discussion of it in *The Mutual Flame* (pp. 49 f.). I agree with Mr Knight that the subject here is Shakespeare's homosexual experience, but cannot accept his contention, which he makes clear by his paraphrase, that it represents an apology for the homo- or bi-sexual transcendentalism of poetic genius. The problem Shakespeare deals with is solely that of how he regards public condemnation; it is not at all one of private poetic conscience. By its great subtlety of thought this sonnet separates the realist's admission of his pleasure in 'vice', and the cynic's hypocritical pursuit of it. It exposes the heartless cynicism that is at the root of public 'morality'.
1-4. These lines, which provide an example of poetic precision unparalleled by few save Shakespeare himself, defy accurate paraphrase – as the many attempts of commentators show. However, the essential meaning is: 'Vice consists of experiencing sensations which are said to be disgusting; so if you become the victim of scandal you might just as well experience them anyway, since in a sense – as you have been branded as vicious when you were not so – they are your due. After all, it is only from the gossips' superficial point of view that these sensations are disgusting. You might find you like them very much'. Shakespeare's experience may well have closely resembled this: having become the subject of scandal through no fault of his own, he then proceeded to 'be vile'. 'Why should I be dragged down to the level of those who judge what they have heard of my amorous exploits by their own coarse and inferior sexual natures?'
6. *give salutation to*: variously glossed, as 'excite', 'affect', 'stir and so infect',

'recognize', 'tempt'. The most accurate equivalent is that of Neilson and Hill (ed. 1942): 'Treat as akin (to their baseness)'.
7-8. What Shakespeare is announcing is that he is independent of other people in his private life, since he is more serious, thorough and reflective. 'Why should less serious people than myself', he is asking, 'influence my opinion of myself?'
9. *I am that I am*: Thus implying the continuation, 'unlike my hypocritical and secretly lascivious detractors, I do not base my view of what I have done, or of what anybody else does, upon a false and spurious morality'. By his poetic independence and lack of pretence, Shakespeare proudly dissociates himself from all superficial criticism – and thus, for those who wish to hear – silences for ever the hypocritical voice of moral opprobrium. *levell*: see 117, 11, n.
11. *straight*: not 'virtuous', but merely 'straightforward'. *bevel*: literally. 'oblique, sloping'; here, the equivalent of the modern slang, 'crooked' or 'bent'. Steevens (ed. 1780) glossed this as a mason's and joiner's exclusive term for 'crooked', which it still is.
12-14. 'My deeds could truly be considered only in the light of what such people think or say if I, as well as my actions, resembled them to the extent of upholding the cynical principle by which they live; namely, that all men are inherently bad, and should prosper and exult in their evil.'

122

1. *tables*: memorandum-book – Pooler's suggestion (ed. 1918) is worth quoting: '... perhaps "the vacant leaves" of 77 filled with his friend's thoughts... read... by Shakespeare and now given away'.
3. *that idle rancke*: that mere perishable note-book. 'Rancke' is literally 'movement in line or file', and here applies to the writing in the note-book.
6. 'Are able by nature to remain alive'.
7. *raz'd oblivion*: oblivion which leaves nothing behind.
9. *poore retention*: this refers to the tables (in contrast to the memory within Shakespeare's brain).
10. *tallies*: sticks upon which scores in card-games, etc., were registered by means of notches.
12. *those tables*: my memory.
13. *adjunckt*: something like the note-book (or any other material remembrance of you).
14. *import*: betoken. indicate.

123

G. Wilson Knight writes perceptively in *The Mutual Flame*: 'An uneasy sonnet... written by a man who knows his love is changing, but who refuses to believe that

the essence of it is lost'.
2. *pyramyds*: anything that Time erects to impress.
3. *nothing... nothing*: may be read either as adverbs, 'not at all', or as nouns.
4. There is nothing truly new. In other words, human nature is not changed, nor is Time really so mighty that it can change it. *dressings*: repetition, in a different form, of things which have existed in former times.
5-6. Time is described as a kind of trickster; or rather, essentially, those who think of Time as all-powerful are described as its superficial gulls. ' We have such short lives that we are taken in by Time, which presents eternal things as novelties.'
7-8. 'We prefer to regard what is impressive in our own times as new and created by ourselves, rather than to remember what we know – that past ages achieved just as much.'
11-12. 'Everything we see is distorted – magnified or diminished – by the continual passage of Time, and by our dependence on it.'

124

1-4. 'If my love had arisen from mere circumstance, then it would have ceased as soon as it became unprofitable; it would have gone the way of all flesh, subject to the caprices of time and fortune.'
5. 'It arose from something permanent and eternal, in contrast to the accidents of time.'
11. Shakespeare sees his own love (and the general power of love) as something standing against the transitory material values; it influences his action, and therefore may truthfully be described as 'hugely pollitick'.
13-14. 'The foles of time' are, in Shakespeare, everyone: since Shakespeare's characters, as has been pointed out in connection with these lines, are 'fooled' by Time. But some of them have sacrificed or destroyed themselves for more eternal values; Shakespeare here calls them as witnesses to his own attitude, which, being an anti-materialist one, might seem priggish, hypocritical or even impossible. The reference is almost certainly to those who have died for their religious beliefs; but it is 'policy' that is the true heretic.

125

The first twelve lines of this sonnet answer the imaginary accusation of the 'subbornd *Informer'* of l. 13; this is Shakespeare's justification of the anti-materialistic attitude of the preceding sonnets. The paradox he must keep nagging at is that his relationship with the Friend, who is worthless, has been a physical one, and yet only through this very fact has he been able to reach his present emotional state. The thoughtless celebration of the external beauty of youth, of which Shakespeare sees himself accused here, is a metaphor for his previous dependence upon it. The whole sonnet recalls 119, 9-12. The 'subbornd *Informer*' is almost certainly the Friend himself.

1-4. 'Would it have profited me if I had honoured my friend's physical beauty in verse, or if I had attempted to create immortality out of something which has a brief duration?' Persons of rank were entitled to have a canopy borne over them; here the term is a metaphor for 'to honour'. The 'great bases for eternity' are to be equated with Time's 'pyramyds buylt up with newer might', whose impressiveness Shakespeare rejects in 123. He rejects both courses as poetically unprofitable.

5. *dwellers... favor*: those who rely on outward manifestations of admiration.

7. *compound sweet*: this refers to the mixture of 'forme and favor' which those who have lost all have relied upon.

7-8. *Forgoing... spent*: 'They have eschewed the simple private enjoyment of a loved one in favour of the ill-advised fawning of courtiers.'

9. 'No, let me be dutiful to you only privately, and according to my private standards.'

11. *seconds*: the inferior flour that is left after sieving. Shakespeare means that his oblation to the Friend is unmixed with inferior or public motives.

12. *render*: a play on 'surrender' (me to you, and you to me), and the legal sense meaning a 'return'. *onely*: simply.

13-14. The Friend himself is the accuser, and although Shakespeare has been at pains to show that he loves him in his fashion, he is also concerned to show that he is no longer 'in his control'. These lines attempt to remind the Friend of something which he has clearly never understood.

126

Written as a final farewell, the lines do not, of course, constitute a sonnet – except in the sense that any brief lyric was called a sonnet in Shakespeare's time. They may have been intended as a tail-piece.

1-2. *in... hould*: because of his beauty and potential virtue, to which Shakespeare has so often alluded. *fickle glasse, his sickle, hower*: Numerous emendations have been made with regard to this. The most sensible is 'times fickle glasse, his tickle hower', with 'tickle' in its meaning of 'inconstant'. Good sense can be made of Q, however, despite its clumsiness. The lovely boy holds three things in his power: Time's fickle looking-glass (with an appropriate play on Time's traditional hour-glass), Time's sickle (with which it destroys) and Time's 'hour', i.e. Time's power to determine things, chiefly the time of death. In 1893 a correspondent to *Notes and Queries*, defending Q, wrote: ' "Hour" has a particular application, as in the phrase "the hour has come".' This means that the youth has the powers of immortality and can triumph over Time.

3. *wayning growne*: grown more beautiful as you have grown older.
5. *wrack*: destruction.
6. Nature keeps the youth beautiful despite his passing years. (But Shakespeare goes on to remind him that she has a purpose in this.)
7-8. She is not preserving him for his sake, but for the sake of confounding Time's dominion over her.
9. *minnion*: darling, favourite.
10. *still*: always.
11. *Audite*: final account.
12. *Quietus*: (i) acquittance (a legal term, short for *quietus est* = he is quit, i.e. has made settlement); (ii) discharge from life, peace. *render*: surrender (you to Time).

127

This sonnet begins a new series, 127-152, most of which concern Shakespeare's mistress (see Introduction). In this sonnet 'blacke' is used in three senses: 'ugliness', 'wickedness' (= the moral ugliness of artificially induced beauty), 'swarthiness of complexion'. The basic argument regarding his mistress is: 'While so many women to-day, who are not truly beautiful, make themselves seem so by artificial means, my mistress, who is not good-looking, makes herself appear so in everyone's eyes because she does not resort to artificial means – because she is her natural self.' The immediate inference to be drawn, of course, is of a spiritual beauty, of naturalness, informing and transforming her plainness. But there are hints of a different nature: she *is* black, i.e. wicked; she *is* ugly; and she does not do so badly by her eccentricity (of not 'painting'), since 'every tongue' esteems her as a prototype of beauty. Thus, she is described at the outset, with great subtlety and precision, as a woman whose considerable personal magnetism lies not in her appearance but in her strong-willed refusal to alter it. Shakespeare evinces great admiration for her in these lines, but he already exercises a notable restraint: something is withheld. The nature of this restraint is made evident only in the sonnets following.
1-4. 'In times gone by swarthiness was not regarded as beautiful, or if it were privately, it never was in public; but nowadays it has become the prototype of beauty, and thus true Beauty (of the old type) is slandered because it has become suspect.' There is a pun involved between 'blacke' and 'faire' in its senses of 'beautiful' and 'blond'.
5-8. 'For since every woman now uses cosmetics – concealing her ugliness with a lie that is even of her own invention – true Beauty has to hide itself for fear of being regarded as something disgraceful, and is neither honoured nor idolized as it should be.' Shakespeare appears to regard blondness as the prototype of true beauty; but he is probably only taking up an attitude.
9-14. These difficult lines are a paradox; the meaning becomes clearer when we

realize that there is a play on 'faire' every time it appears in this sonnet. The lady's raven eyes are mourning for those who paint to appear 'faire' (both blonde and beautiful – which she does not). In their *natural* blackness and mourning they are so becoming that they convert people to her own swarthiness and 'every toung saies beauty should looke so'.

128

Ostensibly a pretty sonnet to his lady playing the virginals, and certainly a relatively slight piece; but there is a case for suggesting that it may be rather more than it seems. The jack was 'an upright piece of wood fixed to the keylever and fitted with a quill that plucked the string as the jack rose when the key was pressed down' (Onions), but it is generally and sensibly conceded that Shakespeare here meant the wooden keys themselves. However, this was by no means the only meaning of Jack': it meant, among other things, 'any common fellow', 'a low knave', and it was frequently in use as a term of contempt. I suggest that there is an extensive pun involved: the 'Jackes', upon which the lady 'plays', represent the fellows whom she allows to pay court to her, and who, unlike Shakespeare, are not 'serious', but are 'bold', 'dead wood' (i.e. 'blockish') and 'sausie'. Thus, he wraps up his anxiety about her intentions; and ends the sonnet with a pretty, conventional compliment. There is a gentle, though hidden, reproach involved.

1. *my musike*: a complimentary term. *blessed*: by being touched by your fingers.
3. *swayst*: directs, controls.
4. *confounds*: the primary meaning is 'gives delight to', but there is a play on the sense 'confuses'.
5. *envie*: the accent must be on the second syllable. *Jackes*: See above.
11. *gate*: gait.

129

1-2. *Th'expence... action*: 'Lust in action' represents a squandering of spiritual energy in a void of guilt and shame. This is a very accurate psychological observation: a person turns desperately to the expression of lust in order to dissipate a general feeling of unease, brought on by feelings of guilt and shame. Pooler's explanation, 'Loss of vitality by waste that brings discredit' represents a secondary meaning, but is superficial – the sonnet is not about discredit. *and till action*: Shakespeare goes on to enumerate what 'the world well knowes' to be true, and yet cannot shun. *Spirit*: a brilliant sexual pun.
3. *perjurd*: corrupt: lying in order to get its way. *blouddy full of blame*: passionately full of hatred.
4. *rude*: brutal. *not to trust*: treacherous.

6. *past reason hunted*: pursued without any reasonable consideration of the consequences.
7-8. 'It is unreasonable to hate lust as something deliberately laid down to trap you and send you mad; a reasonable man would blame only himself.'
9-10. 'A person is mad both when anticipating it and when expressing it; the extremes of lust are felt after its performance, during it, and in pursuit of it.' (Graves and Riding in *A Survey of Modernist Poetry*, reprinted in *The Common Asphodel* by Robert Graves, 1950, defend the Q punctuation in these lines, in the course of a remarkable analysis of this sonnet, designed to show how modern editorial interference has changed the meaning.) The line is usually, and unnecessarily, emended to: 'Had, having, and in quest to have, extreme.'
11. 'Blissful while it is being experienced, but producing exactly the opposite effect afterwards.'
14. *heaven*: refers to the 'blisse in proofe'.

130

This is not intended to disparage the Mistress's looks, as so many commentators have understood; Shakespeare means that she and her looks, taken together, do not require such ridiculous comparisons. He is satirizing the 'poetical' insincerity of some of his contemporaries, and more particularly the attitude of mind that went with it. At the same time, his insistence upon the Mistress's total independence of all 'poetical' praise adds up to the wry suggestion that she is not conventionally good-looking in any sense at all: her attraction for him is based on something unusual. As Wilson Knight writes in *The Mutual Flame*: 'it appears to have been finer than lust and cruder than love'.
5. *damaskt*: this seems here to mean 'variegated, of a mingled red and white'; but O.E.D. and Onions, citing this line, give 'having the hue of the damask rose'.
8. *reekes*: is emitted or exhaled. The sense of 'stinks' was unknown to Shakespeare.
12. This does not mean that the Mistress had flat feet, but simply that she is a real woman – and that therefore none of her attributes are imaginary.
14. There is a *double entendre* in this line, hinging on the meanings of 'she'. Primarily, 'she' here is a noun meaning 'woman', i.e. Shakespeare thinks his mistress is as beautiful ('rare') as any of the women who have been the subject of extravagant and false comparisons. But 'she' may also refer to his Mistress, and thus the line may yield up the odd but intelligible meaning: 'I think my mistress quite as exceptional ("rare") as any of those whom she has calumniated.' In the second meaning, which is really no more than an undertone, the phrase 'by heaven' implies 'because of my lust' (see 129, 14, for 'heaven' in this application). But Shakespeare may not refer merely to a habit of calumny towards others that the Mistress may be used to exercising: there is a sense in which her 'mourning' for

the artificial beauties in 127 is 'false', for is she not herself 'black'? (See 127, 9-14, n.)

131

1. *tiranous*: pitiless, cruel. *so as thou art*: being, as you are, dark and not fair (and therefore having no claim to beauty).
2. 'With the sense of rightful pride felt by those who have no claim to beauty.'
3-4. In other words, Shakespeare is accusing the Mistress of tyrannizing over him only because she is secure in her sway over him.
5. *in good faith*: This is not an expletive, as most editors take it to be, altering Q to 'Yet, in good faith'; it refers to the good faith of the Mistress's detractors, as Wyndham noted in his edition of 1898.
7-8. Shakespeare dare not assert this in public, presumably because, as Rollins points out in his *New Variorum* edition of 1944, the detractors believe, like the people of times gone by, that 'black' is 'not counted fair'.
10. *but thinking on*: 'when I merely think of (let alone actually see)'.
11. *One... necke*: one (groan) after another, in quick succession.
13. *blacke*: here used to mean 'ugly'; in 1. 12 it means 'dark-complexioned',
14. *slaunder*: this must refer to lines 5-6.

132

As Miss Bradbrook writes *in Shakespeare and Elizabethan Poetry,* the manner here is borrowed 'quite shamelessly' from Sidney, *Astrophel and Stella*, vii.
1-4. 'I love your eyes because, knowing that your heart despises me, they pity me and look lovingly upon my sufferings.' (Shakespeare's own heart and eye had been 'at a mortall warre' in 46). The quality of the Mistress's attraction for Shakespeare consists partly of its 'mourning' aspect. *torment*: usually emended to 'torments'; but as Tucker writes, 'the word is infinitive; cf. e.g. "I have known her torment him".'
5-9. In these lines the notion of his Mistress's 'mourning' quality is developed further. Does she compensate Shakespeare physically for her failure to love him? 138 provides the answer to this. There is, of course, a play on 'mourning' in lines 5 and 9; most editors actually emend to 'mourning' in 1. 9, but Q as usual is better: 'morning eyes' directly suggests the nature of her compassion – Shakespeare is telling us that he was familiar with her eyes as she awoke. Rollins states that here Shakespeare 'makes the "false compare" at which he had mocked in 130'; but it is clear that he was engaged in saying something quite different.
10-12. The sense of this difficult passage is: 'Please continue your "mourning" for me, in view of its nature; you make love as though you meant it, so please try to mean it in reality.' *sute thy pitty like in every part*: literally, means: 'dress

every part of you (i.e. not only your eyes, but also your heart) in keeping with your mourning'.
13-14. Shakespeare has in effect asked his Mistress to love him as well as sleep with him, since she does the latter so convincingly; if she does, he says, he will go so far as to elevate her to the position of a prototype of beauty – something he has previously (131, 7) said he would not dare to do.

133

Rollins is right in saying (ed. 1944) that 'comparatively few persons have agreed with' Beeching's statement (ed. 1904) that 'this sonnet treats, from the woman's point of view, the same subject as sonnets… 40-42'; however, the introduction of a new 'friend', when 133-134 fit so well into the psychological picture given by the previous sonnets, is not such an easy matter. Beeching and Butler, who placed these sonnets much earlier in the sequence, are more likely to be correct. My own suggestion is that Shakespeare wrote these at roughly the same time as 40-42, but, because they were addressed to his Mistress and not to the Friend, as 40-42 are, he included them with the other sonnets of the series 127-152. This may not make chronological sense, but it makes good poetic sense. (There is no reason to suppose that *all* the sonnets to his Mistress were not written contemporaneously with the ones to the Friend; when Shakespeare had finished writing sonnets, he divided those that dealt primarily with the Friend from those that dealt primarily with the Mistress.)
4. In order to be Shakespeare's friend, the Friend must be a 'slave' (friend) to 'slavery' (Shakespeare's condition).
5. She has distracted Shakespeare.
6. *my next selfe*: my friend. *ingrossed*: monopolized (i.e. he is grumbling because she has not only divided him against himself, but also taken his friend from him – see 1. 7).
10. *bale*: here means 'confine'.
11. *garde*: guard-room or house.
12-14. 'Then (if I still have friend's love) you cannot torture me in my prison; and yet you can – for you own all of me, including what I love.' Shakespeare here seems to acknowledge the greater power of his Mistress.

134

1. As explained in 133.
2. *will*: (i) lust; (ii) purpose, desire. (There may be a further play intended, of course, if the Friend's name was Will.)
3-4. 'I will give myself up to you, provided you will give my friend up to me.' ('So' here means 'provided that'.)

5. 'But you will not give him up, nor does he wish you to.'
7-8. Presumably the Friend had acted in some capacity for Shakespeare, and had then been persuaded to take over his functions. (See 40, 5-6.)
9. *statute*: 'Bond by virtue of which "the Creditor may immediately have execution upon the Debtor's Body, Land and Goods".' (Onions.)
10. *use*: See 6, 5, n. But the line also has an obvious sexual connotation.
11. *came*: who became.
12. *unkinde abuse*: 'my unnatural and unkind practice' (of asking him to act for me). (Or this may mean: 'through your unkind treatment of me' – "my" meaning, "inflicted upon me".)
114. *He paies the whole*: this implies that the Friend is at present monopolizing the Mistress in a physical sense.

135

This sonnet strongly suggests that the 'friend' of 133 and 134 – whoever – he may have been (see Introduction) – was known as 'Will'. It would read very flatly otherwise. Apart from this conjectural but likely meaning the word, is played upon here in four other senses: (i) Shakespeare's own Christian name; (ii) lust, sexual desire; (iii) penis ('willy' is a well-authenticated term of schoolboy slang, still in use to my own knowledge); (iv) in a direct physical sense, applying to the Mistress, through a natural extension of its meaning of 'lust, sexual desire'. (Line 5 makes this abundantly clear.)
1. Lee (*Life of Shakespeare*, 1898) calls this first line 'a slight variation on the current catch-phrase "a woman will have her will" '. When the fourth meaning (listed above) of 'will' is read into it, it is plainly derogatory.
5-8. Evidently the Mistress enjoyed denying Shakespeare her favours, though she was so free with them to others.
13. Commentators have had great trouble with this puzzling line; Dowden's reading (1881), 'Let no unkinde "No" faire beseechers kill' is probably correct, and has the advantage of not interfering with Q – the comma is demanded by the rhythm.
13-14. 'Do not refuse *anyone* (including me): think of them as all the same, since they bear the same name – and further, as that is my name as well, think of them all as me.' By punningly equating the names of the Mistress's suitors with 'lust', Shakespeare emphasizes both the nature of his own attachment and the Mistress's fundamental sensuality.

136

This repeats the argument of the final couplet in 135 in more detail.
1. *come so neere*: am so familiar with you.

2. *Sweare to thy blind soule*: 'Swear to your soul, which has not physical eyes to see'. *thy* Will: refers to the Friend, unless there is a third Will involved, namely the Mistress's husband or established lover.
3. *will*: used in the third of the senses enumerated in the introduction to 135. This is not complimentary to the quality of her soul. *admitted there*: to her 'large and spacious' 'will'. This is, of course, highly uncomplimentary.
5. Will: used primarily in the second of the senses already enumerated; but the italics emphasize his argument (that the Mistress should accept him because of his name and what it means).
6. *I*: ay.

137

The situation described here is in one sense similar to that of 113, where Shakespeare could see nothing but the image of the Friend: now his eyes take the 'worst' to be the 'best'. His difficulty is a perhaps familiar one: where he desires, he cannot help loving – and, naturally enough, he suspects the quality of such love.
5-8. This means: 'Why, because I desire and enjoy this woman physically, should I have to *love* her?'
9. *severall plot*: an exclusive pasture, for the use of one person only; the opposite of 'common' (l. 10).
11. *not*: universally (except by Harrison, ed. 1937) emended to 'not,'. But Shakespeare means: 'Why, seeing that my heart treats my Mistress as though she were not a whore, though knowing she is one, do not my eyes say that this is merely in order to pretend that what is foul is fair?'
13. This seems to refer to the state of mind described in 113.

138

In the first (1599) edition of *The Passionate Pilgrim* (see Introduction) this sonnet runs thus:

When my Love sweares that she is made of truth,
I do beleeve her (though I know she lies)
That she might thinke me some untuter'd youth,
Unskilful in the worlds false forgeries.
Thus vainly thinking that she thinkes me young,
Although I know my yeares be past the best:
I smiling, credite her false speaking toung,
Outfacing faults in love, with loves ill rest.
But wherefore sayes my love that she is young?

And wherefore say not I, that I am old:
O, Loves best habit's in a soothing toung,
And Age in love, loves not to have yeares told.
  Therefore I'le lye with Love, and love with me,
  Since that our faultes in love thus smother'd be.

The 1612 version resembles this except in two unimportant details.

It has been suggested that the *Passionate Pilgrim* version is a reconstruction of the Q text from memory; but if anything looks like an earlier draft, this does.

For the first time in the series addressed to the Mistress, Shakespeare deals directly and 'sympathetically' with the physical nature of their odd and cryptic relationship. As Miss Mahood writes in *Shakespeare's Wordplay*, '...the total impression... is not one of bitterness, but of acceptance. The lovers need one another in their common weakness'. Shakespeare is here less hard on himself and the Mistress than he is in 137; the conclusion explains why he 'believes' what he knows to be false.

1. *sweares*: This 'swearing'– the untrue but accepted affirmations on both sides – is all done in the course of making love, of 'lying'. Part of the point of the sonnet – and probably what occasioned it – is the need sensitive people have to talk like this while making illicit love. It provides a kind of comfort, a semi-hysterical insulation against their own feelings of guilt and dishonesty.

2. 'I accept what she says at its face-value, without reproaching her, though I know it to be untrue.'

6. This line has troubled commentators, since Shakespeare could not have been more than 35 when he wrote it. But in the first draft he wrote: '*I* know my yeares, etc.' Probably he was thinking of the contrasting youth of the Friend or of the Mistress's other suitors, and comparing his own performance, perhaps inhibited by some of the scruples he reveals in the sonnets to her, with theirs.

14. *faults*: as Miss Mahood observes, this is used in two senses: their infidelities to one another, and their faults of character. *flattered*: primarily used in the sense of 'deluded', but also means 'coddled, gratified, encouraged'.

139

By comparison, this is a trivial piece.

1. Poetical, if not poetic, convention demanded that Shakespeare should justify it.

3. He asks her to tell him outright, and not play at being 'distant' with him.

4. *Art*: artfulness, cunning.

7. *What*: why.

9-12. The 'excuse' is: 'She knows that her "looks" have made me suffer with love (or desire) for her, therefore she is casting them in other directions to spare me.'

140

3. *Least*: lest.
4. *pittie wanting paine*: pain which desires to be pitied.
5. *witte*: wisdom. *weare*: were.
11. *ill wresting*: to strain the meaning of, towards the worst.
13. *belyde*: lied about.
14. *goe wide*: go wide of the mark.

141

This sonnet is frequently taken as proof that the Mistress was an ugly woman; but as Rollins (ed. 1944) writes, '... Shakespeare's comments... appear to be motivated by anguish at the woman's falseness to himself... He seems much more bothered by the irrationality of his obsession than about her ill colour.' This irrationality seems to have consisted of a physical need for her which was not, however, physically inspired. It is true that Shakespeare states that he does not desire a 'sensuall feast' with her, but in view of what he clearly says in other sonnets, it is obvious that he is pointing out that his lust for her is not an ordinary lust – is not inspired by looking at her. He could only escape from his loathing of lust, it appears, by indulging in it with this woman: however 'black' her deeds may have been, she possessed some quality of understanding, or some awareness, which was necessary to Shakespeare, and that he unwillingly admired.
4. *Who*: refers to 'heart'. See also l. 11.
6. He means that he is not susceptible to mere 'sexiness'.
11-12. He becomes 'the likenesse of a man' (i.e. one without a heart), while his heart becomes the vassal of the Mistress.
13-14. The 'sin' is presumably the same kind of lying as Shakespeare accused himself of in the final couplet of 113 (see n.). 'Paine' here means deserved punishment, for which he is poetically grateful; but Tucker notes that 'the "pain" which *she* awards is... not without its gratifications'.

142

It becomes clear here that the Mistress's contempt for Shakespeare arises from his professions of 'love' for her when in fact, from her point of view, he needs her only physically. It is her 'point of view' which both fascinates and repels Shakespeare; plainly what she fails to understand – and it has baffled readers of the sonnets ever since – is the peculiar quality of his feeling for her (as expressed, in particular, in 141).

1. *deare*: used primarily in a combination of two of its meanings: 'especial' and 'unusual'; but the hate is poetically valuable to Shakespeare because it 'awards him pain', and it is therefore 'dear' to him.

2. *grounded... loving*: this has been variously interpreted, but is a genuine ambiguity. It means: (i) 'Your hate is (rightly) grounded upon the sinful (i.e. primarily lustful) nature of my loving'. (ii) 'Your hate arises from your promiscuous nature'. Both these are true, and the one reinforces the other.

6-7. *prophan'd... love*: Malone (ed. 1790) drew attention to the phrase 'scarlet ornaments' (for blushes) in a play, *The Reign of King Edward the Third* (1596, of unknown authorship). But it has been pointed out that here the phrase refers to the scarlet wax with which the bond of l. 7 is sealed. More generally, it implies that she has used her beauty falsely.

9. Means that he has the right to love her in his way just as she has to be naturally promiscuous.

11-12. 'Become a compassionate person so that you yourself may deserve compassion.'

13-14. This hints that the Mistress eschews compassion for her lovers as a deliberate policy; Shakespeare is not asking for her full love but for a fuller and perhaps kinder relationship. 'Hide' is possibly used in its sense of 'protect'.

143

Steevens (ed. 1780) wrote of this sonnet: 'The image with which... [it]... begins, is at once pleasing and natural; but the conclusion of it is lame and impotent indeed. We attend to the cries of the infant, but laugh at the loud blubberings of the great boy Will.' This, of course, is a splendid example of hitting the nail on the head by missing it. Clearly the Mistress regarded Shakespeare's feelings for her as soft and blubbering; and to some extent Shakespeare agreed with her.

1. *carefull*: 'attentive', with a play on the sense of 'full of anxiety'.

5. *holds... chace*: pursues her.

13. *Will*: This may be a play on the name of the man she was chasing at the time – probably on that of the Friend (see notes to 135, 136). But chiefly Shakespeare means that she can have her will (of him as well as of anyone else she fancies) so long as she cares for him, and gives him the compassion about which he has written in the preceding sonnet.

144

This sonnet also appeared in *The Passionate Pilgrim* (see introduction to 138), and as with 138, is clearly an improved later draft. This is the 1599 *Passionate Pilgrim* version, which differs from that of 1612 only in a few slight details of spelling:

Two loves I have, of Comfort and Despaire,
That like two Spirits, do suggest me still:
My better Angell, is a Man (right faire)
My worser spirit a Woman (colour'd ill).
To win me soone to hell, my Female evill
Tempteth my better Angell from my side:
And would corrupt my Saint to be a Divell,
Wooing his puritie with her faire pride.
And whether that my Angell be turnde feend,
Suspect I may (yet not directly tell:)
For being both to me: both, to each friend,
I guesse one Angell in anothers hell:
  The truth I shall not know, but live in dout,
  Till my bad Angell fire my good one out.

1. H. Littledale wrote in *Shakespeare's England* (1916): 'The Church inculcated belief in the good genius or guardian angel, told off to watch over every human soul, and also in the hosts of evil spirits who strove... to thwart the good angel's gracious ministrations. In (Marlowe's) *Faustus* these opposing powers exhort Faustus alternately... ' The 'despair' is largely that of 129.
2. *sugiest*: suggest: 'tempt', or 'prompt towards comfort or despair'.
5-8. Shakespeare would be 'won to hell' if the Friend were turned into a 'fiend' (see 1. 9).
9-10. The Friend has 'turned fiend' if he is sleeping with the Mistress: first, because he would be entering into a purely physical relationship; secondly, because he would be deceiving Shakespeare.
11. 'But both being estranged from me, close to one another.'
12. A. Forbes Sieveking quotes this description of the game of Barley-break, or Last-in-hell, in *Shakespeare's England* (1916): 'It was played by six persons, three of each sex, coupled by lot. A piece of ground is divided into three compartments, the middle one being called "hell". The couple condemned to hell try to catch the others advancing from the extremities; if they succeed, the hell-pair change places with the couple taken. In the catching, the middle pair were not to separate before they succeeded, while the others might loose hands at any time if pressed. When all had been taken the last couple was said to be "in hell", and the game ended: Hussey's assertion (ed. 1888) that this line contains a reference to Barley-break has been challenged; but lines 5-7 seem to bear him out. 'Hell' also has here an obvious physical connotation.
14. *fire... out*: as Rollins (ed. 1944) points out, this has the meaning of 'communicate a venereal disease'. Shakespeare will not know for certain if the Friend is sleeping with the Mistress until he displays symptoms of venereal disease. (To 'fire out' also refers to the custom of smoking a fox out of its lair by making a

fire at one end of it.) This is indeed disgusting and insulting; but it is that very aspect of it which offers the clue to Shakespeare's true feelings. By taking the Mistress, the Friend will become corrupt and diseased: will no longer represent purity for Shakespeare. Yet in seeking the total meaning of this sonnet, we must take into account Shakespeare's own sexual 'use' of the Mistress; and we must remember that, in speaking of his 'good' and 'bad' angels, he is referring to the elements of 'love' and 'lust' within himself. Thus l. 12 could also mean that love, in himself, is trapped in and threatened by a hell of lust. Yet it is by the practice of lust that love can be brought into the open (see introduction to 123).

145

Commentators have mostly rejected this, either as un-Shakespearean or clearly not about the Mistress. There is no good reason, however, why it should not be about her; and it makes a pleasant enough interlude in this waste of shame. It is nearer to the sonnet-form than 128, being regular in all respects except that it is in tetrameters instead of pentameters.

146

While this has no connection with the 'story' behind the sonnets, it arises from it.
2. *Gull'd by*: Malone (ed. 1780) was almost certainly correct in surmising that the lost three words of l. 1 were inadvertently repeated. His own often adopted emendation 'fool'd by' is probably the best of the score or so of suggested ones, but as conjecture is free here, I have preferred my own guess. 'Gull'd by' has, in my view, the slightly stronger meaning of 'duped' that is demanded by the context. Other emendations worthy of note are: 'Feeding these' (Sebastian Evans), 'Bearing these' (Harrison), 'Trick'd by' (Latham Davis), 'Starv'd by (the)' (Steevens) and 'Fenced by' (Sisson). *array*: clothe.
9. 'Live, soul, upon the privations of your servant, the body.'
10. pine: want. *aggravat*: add to, increase.
11. *tearmes divine*: eternity.
13-14. 'By depriving the body, the soul is depriving death, which feeds upon the body; thus death will be starved and die, and the soul will enjoy immortality.' Shakespeare means that if the pursuit of material happiness can be given up, then the fear of losing it, of death, vanishes. There is no reason for according a specifically 'Christian' interpretation to this sonnet, as has frequently been suggested.

147

1-2. His love for the Mistress is compared to a feverish delirium which seeks to perpetuate itself.
4. *uncertaine... appetite*: i.e. of his love.
7. *approove*: confirm.
8. *except*: object to.
12. *randon*: random.

148

Like 113 and 137, this is on the theme of love's distortion of 'sight'; but here Shakespeare gives more justification for this state (l. 12). He also, by implication, acquits love of the guilt of being a distorter of truth: it is the 'tears' – the self-centred grief felt by the lover at the pain inflicted upon him – that distort truth.
8. There is a pun involved here, as the line may be read: 'Love's "ay" is not so true as all men's "no" ': But the rhythm, pointed by the colon after 'men's', indicates the primary meaning.
10. *watching*: wakefulness.

149

This continues and develops the theme of 142 (see introduction to that sonnet).
2. This is not at all the same kind of self-enmity as is expressed in 49 and 88. Here, Shakespeare refers to the fact that he goes to bed with the Mistress; clearly she laughs at him for wanting to make any more of their relationship than this.
4. *all... sake*: made into a tyrant over myself for your sake.
9-10. 'What quality do I look up to in myself that would despise to serve you?'
13-14. The Mistress loves those who can 'see straight' (i.e. those who do not make more fuss about lust than is strictly necessary); Shakespeare, as he has said in 148, is 'blind' in this respect.

150

2. 'To dominate my heart by means of, not despite, your shortcomings.'
4. An allusion to the Mistress's 'blackness' or 'ill-colour'.
5. 'From where do you obtain your faculty of making ugliness have grace ('becomming')?
7. *warrantise*: guarantee. *skill*: wisdom and mental power.
13-14. If Shakespeare unworthily loves the Mistress for her unworthiness, then all the more reason for her to love him.

151

Like 20, this sonnet has been described as 'gross', 'sickly and nauseous', 'packed with ribaldry' and 'one which, from the nature of its contents, might well be let die'. However, the 'rising and falling' is singularly appropriate to its theme of involuntary lust; the point is that it is *not* a metaphor.

1. *conscience*: in its usual sense; also, as Tucker pointed out (ed. 1924): 'guilty "knowing" '. The sense of the whole line is both 'love is too tender, too innocent a thing to know the meaning of guilt' and 'love is too foolish to understand the guilty consequences to which it leads'.

2. *conscience... love*: both 'guilt only comes from love' and 'conscience (in its usual sense of "faculty distinguishing between good and evil") is only created by having experienced love.'

3. *cheater*: deceiver. *my amisse*: presumably this is what the Mistress has accused Shakespeare of in 149.

6. Literally, his spirit is betrayed by the involuntary movement of his flesh.

7. *may*: as Simpson points out (*Shakespearian Punctuation*), this pause is rhythmical.

8. *reason*: discourse.

152

3-4. 'You are false to your previous lover (possibly husband) in sleeping with me; and you are false to me in vowing hate after having vowed love.'

7. *misuse thee*: 'misrepresent you (by saying you are beautiful, which is false)'.

9. *deepe*: solemn.

13. *eye*: always emended to 'I', but refers – with, of course, a pun involved – to 'eyes' of l. 11.

153

Both this and 154 are poor sonnets, having no connection, either in quality or theme, with 1-152. But this is no reason to suppose that they are not by Shakespeare; all that may be said is that there is nothing in them to suggest they are. J. A. K. Thomson *writes* (*Shakespeare and the Classics*): 'CLIII and CLIV are thought to be free renderings of a poem by a certain Marianus... in... the Greek Anthology. It may be so; but the authenticity of these two sonnets is so doubtful, that it would be quite unsafe to use them in evidence... yet anyone who knows the fertility of the Renaissance in the invention of conceits about Cupid will... hesitate before deciding that the fancy... expressed... could not have occurred to an Elizabethan poet independently.'

1. *brand*: torch.

6. *datelesse*: see 30, 6, n. lively: *living*.
7. *seething*: boiling.
12. *distemperd*: out-of-sorts, deranged.

154

A variation on 153.
7. *Generall*: Chief (i.e. Cupid).
13. *this*: refers to the statement in l. 14.

INDEX OF FIRST LINES

References are to sonnet numbers, not page numbers

GREENWICH EXCHANGE BOOKS

STUDENT GUIDES

Greenwich Exchange Student Guides are critical studies of major or contemporary serious writers in English and selected European languages. The series is for the Student, the Teacher and the 'common reader' and are ideal resources for libraries. The *Times Educational Supplement (TES)* praised these books saying "The style of these guides has a pressure of meaning behind it. Students should learn from that... If art is about selection, perception and taste, then this is it."

(ISBN prefix 1-871551- applies)
The series includes:
W. H. Auden by Stephen Wade (-36-6)
William Blake by Peter Davies (-27-7)
The Brontës by Peter Davies (-24-2)
Joseph Conrad by Martin Seymour-Smith (-18-8)
William Cowper by Michael Thorn (-25-0)
Charles Dickens by Robert Giddings (-26-9)
John Donne by Sean Haldane (-23-4)
Thomas Hardy by Sean Haldane (-35-1)
Seamus Heaney by Warren Hope (-37-8)
Philip Larkin by Warren Hope (-35-8)
Tobias Smollett by Robert Giddings (-21-8)
Alfred Lord Tennyson by Michael Thorn (-20-X)
Wordsworth by Andrew Keanie (57-9)

OTHER GREENWICH EXCHANGE BOOKS

All paperbacks unless otherwise stated.

LITERATURE & BIOGRAPHY

Shakespeare's Non-Dramatic Poetry *by Martin Seymour-Smith*
In this study, completed shortly before his death in 1998, Martin Seymour-Smith sheds fresh light on two very different groups of Shakespeare's non-dramatic poems: the early and conventional *Venus and Adonis* and *The Rape of Lucrece*, and the highly personal *Sonnets*. He explains the genesis of the first two in the genre of Ovidian narrative poetry in which a young Elizabethan man of letters was expected to excel, and which was highly popular. In the *Sonnets* (his 1963 old-spelling edition of which is being reissued by Greenwich Exchange) he traces the mental journey of a man going through an acute psychological crisis as he faces up to the truth about his own unconventional sexuality.
It is a study which confronts those "disagreeables" in the *Sonnets* which most critics have ignored.
ISBN 1-871551-22-6; A5 size; 90pp

The Author, the Book & the Reader *by Robert Giddings*
This collection of Essays analyses the effects of changing technology and the attendant commercial pressures on literary styles and subject matter. Authors covered include Dickens; Smollett; Mark Twain; Dr Johnson; John Le Carré.
ISBN 1-871551-01-0; A5 size; 220pp; illus.

In Pursuit of Lewis Carroll *by Raphael Shaberman*
Sherlock Holmes and the author uncover new evidence in their investigations into the mysterious life and writing of Lewis Carroll. They examine published works by Carroll that have been overlooked by previous commentators. A newly discovered poem, almost certainly by Carroll, is published here. Amongst many aspects of Carroll's highly complex personality, this book explores his relationship with his parents, numerous child friends, and the formidable Mrs Liddell, mother of the immortal Alice.
ISBN 1-871551-13-7; 70% A4 size; 130pp; illus.

Norman Cameron *by Warren Hope*
Cameron's poetry was admired by Auden; celebrated by Dylan Thomas; valued by Robert Graves. He was described by Martin Seymour-Smith as one of "... the most rewarding and pure poets of his generation..." and is at last given a full length biography. This eminently sociable man, who had periods of darkness and despair, wrote little poetry by comparison with others of his time, but always of a high and consistent quality - imaginative and profound.
ISBN 1-871551-05-6; A5 size; 250pp; illus.

Liar! Liar!': Jack Kerouac–Novelist *by R. J. Ellis*
The fullest study of Jack Kerouac's fiction to date. It is the first book to devote an individual chapter to each and every one of his novels. *On the Road, Visions of Cody* and *The Subterraneans*, Kerouac's central masterpieces, are reread in-depth, in a new and exciting way. The books Kerouac himself saw as major elements of his spontaneous 'bop' odyssey, *Visions of Gerard* and *Doctor Sax*, are also strikingly reinterpreted, as are other, daringly innovative writings, like 'The Railroad Earth' and his 'try at a spontaneous *Finnegans Wake'*, *Old Angel Midnight*. Undeservedly neglected writings, such as *Tristessa* and *Big Sur*, are also analysed, alongside better known novels like *Dharma Bums* and *Desolation Angels*.
Liar! Liar! takes its title for the words of *Tristessa's* narrator, Jack, referring to himself. He also warns us 'I guess, I'm a liar, watch out!'. R. J. Ellis' study provocatively proposes that we need to take this warning seriously and, rather than reading Kerouac's novels simply as fictional versions of his life, focus just as much on the way the novels stand as variations on a series of ambiguously-represented themes: explorations of class, sexual identity, the French-Canadian Catholic confessional, and addiction in its hydra-headed modern forms. Ellis shows how Kerouac's deep anxieties in each of these arenas makes him an incisive commentator on his uncertain times and a bitingly honest self-critic, constantly

attacking his narrators' 'vanities'.
R. J. Ellis is Professor of English and American Studies at the Nottingham Trent University. His commentaries on Beat writing have been frequently published, and his most recent book, a full modern edition of Harriet Wilson's *Our Nig*, the first ever novel by an African American woman, has been widely acclaimed.
ISBN 1-871551-53-6; A5 size; 300pp

PHILOSOPHY

Marx: Justice and Dialectic *by James Daly*
Department of Scholastic Philosophy, Queen's University, Belfast.
James Daly shows the humane basis of Marx's thinking, rather than the imposed "economic materialistic" views of many modem commentators. In particular he refutes the notion that for Marx, justice relates simply to the state of development of society at a particular time. Marx's views about justice and human relationships belong to the continuing traditions of moral thought in Europe.
ISBN 1-871551-28-5; A5 size; 180 pp

Questions of Platonism *by Ian Leask*
In a daring challenge to contemporary orthodoxy, Ian Leask subverts both Hegel and Heidegger by arguing for a radical re-evaluation of Platonism. Thus, while he traces a profoundly Platonic continuity between ancient Athens and 19th century Germany, the nature of this Platonism, he suggests, is neither 'totalizing' nor Hegelian but, instead, open-ended 'incomplete' and oriented towards a divine goal beyond *logos* or any metaphysical structure. Such a re-evaluation exposes the deep anti-Platonism of Hegel's absolutizing of volitional subjectivity; it also confirms Schelling as true modern heir to the 'constitutive incompletion' of Plato and Plotinus.By providing a more nuanced approach - refusing to accept either Hegel's self-serving account of 'Platonism' or the (equally totalizing) post-Heideggerian inversion of this narrative – Leask demonstrates the continued relevance of a genuine, 'finite' Platonic quest. Ian Leask teaches in the Department of Scholastic Philosophy at the Queen's University of Belfast.
ISBN 1-871551-32-3; A5 size; 154pp

The Philosophy of Whitehead *by T. E. Burke*
Department of Philosophy, University of Reading
Dr Burke explores the main achievements of this philosopher, better known in the US than Britain. Whitehead, often remembered as Russell's tutor and collaborator on *Principia Mathematica,* was one of the few who had a grasp of relativity and its possible implications. His philosophical writings reflect his profound knowledge of mathematics and science. He was responsible for initiating process theology.
ISBN 1-871551-29-3; A5 size; 106pp

POETRY

Lines from the Stone Age *by Sean Haldane*
Reviewing Sean Haldane's 1992 volume *Desire in Belfast* Robert Nye wrote in The *Times* that 'Haldane can be sure of his place among the English poets.' The facts that his early volumes appeared in Canada and that he has earned his living by other means than literature have meant that this place is not yet a conspicuous one, although his poems have always had their circle of readers. The 60 previously unpublished poems of *Lines from the Stone Age* – 'lines of longing, terror, pride, lust and pain' – may widen this circle.
ISBN 1-871551-39-0; A5 size; 58pp

Wilderness *by Martin Seymour-Smith*
This is Seymour-Smith's first publication of his poetry for more than 20 years. This collection of 36 poems is a fearless account of an inner life of love, frustration, guilt, laughter and the celebration of others. Best known to the general public as the author of the controversial and best selling *Hardy* (1994).
ISBN 1-871551-08-0; A5 size; 64pp

Baudelaire: Les Fleurs du Mal in English Verse *translated by F. W. Leakey*
Selected poems from *Les Fleurs du Mal* are translated with parallel French texts, are designed to be read with pleasure by readers who have no French, as well as those practised in the French language.
F. W. Leakey is Emeritus Professor of French in the University of London. As a scholar, critic and teacher he has specialised in the work of Baudelaire for 50 years. He has published a number of books on Baudelaire.
ISBN 1-871551-10-2; A5 size; 140pp

FICTION

The Case of the Scarlet Woman - Sherlock Holmes and the Occult *by Watkin Jones*
A haunted house, a mysterious kidnapping and a poet's demonic visions are just the beginnings of three connected cases that lead Sherlock Holmes into confrontation with the infamous black magician Aleister Crowley and, more sinisterly, his scorned Scarlet Woman.
The fact that Dr Watson did not publish details of these investigations is perhaps testament to the unspoken fear he and Homes harboured for the supernatural. *The Case of the Scarlet Woman* convinced them both that some things cannot be explained by cold logic.
ISBN 1-871551-14-5; A5 size; 130pp

THEATRE

Music Hall Warriors: A history of the Variety Artistes Federation *by Peter Honri*
This is an unique and fascinating history of how vaudeville artistes formed the first effective actor's trade union in 1906 and then battled with the powerful owners of music halls to obtain fairer contracts. The story continues with the VAF dealing with performing rights, radio, and the advent of television. Peter Honri is the fourth generation of a vaudeville family. The book has a foreword by the Right Honourable John Major MP when he was Prime Minister – his father was a founder member of the VAF.
ISBN 1-871551-06-4; A4 size; 140pp; illus.

MISCELLANEOUS

Musical Offering *by Yolanthe Leigh*
In a series of vivid sketches, anecdotes and reflections, Yolanthe Leigh tells the story of her growing up in the Poland of the nineteen thirties and the second world war. These are poignant episodes of a child's first encounters with both the enchantments and the cruelties of the world; and from a later time, stark memories of the brutality of the Nazi invasion, and the hardships of student life in Warsaw under the Occupation. But most of all this is a record of inward development; passages of remarkable intensity and simplicity describe the girl's response to religion, to music, and to her discovery of philosophy.
The outcome is something unique, a book that eludes classification. In its own distinctive fashion, it creates a memorable picture of a highly perceptive and sensitive individual, set against a background of national tragedy.
ISBN 1-871551-46-3; A5 size 61pp